Pathway Through Peril

A Journey of Hope

Inspired by a True Story

Agnes H. Thibert

 FriesenPress

Suite 300 - 990 Fort St
Victoria, BC, V8V 3K2
Canada

www.friesenpress.com

ISBN
978-1-5255-4240-4 (Hardcover)
978-1-5255-4241-1 (Paperback)
978-1-5255-4242-8 (eBook)

1. HISTORY, EUROPE, RUSSIA & THE FORMER SOVIET UNION

Distributed to the trade by The Ingram Book Company

Table of Contents

DEDICATION

To my parents, Anna and Johann Langemann

You told me of your life in another land and showed me the pictures of the loved ones you left behind. In the naivety of youth, I failed to recognize the relevance of your experiences, and yet the stories live on in my memory. Vague and unclear they may be, like a treasured family album with missing chapters or faded pictures. I have tried to fill in the blanks and from my own imagination to reawaken the stories, to pass the album on to my children and grandchildren, in the hopes they see in its pages the narrative of their own past.

ACKNOWLEDGEMENTS

I WISH TO THANK SALLY CONNELLY FOR ENCOURAGING ME TO take the first step on this road to writing discovery, for reading what I produced and giving me her honest and invaluable opinions. A huge thank-you to Tyler Trafford, who from the start of this journey, encouraged, guided, directed and advised, whose faith in my abilities kept me on task when I had my doubts. To Judy Trafford, my gratitude for the wonderful artistic representation of the people who fought their way through the perils of war and revolution. You brought beauty to a dark and ominous landscape.

Thank-you, to my dear children and grandchildren who showed interest and enthusiasm for a project far outside their area of familiarity. It is my hope that each one of you will read this book, whether now or later and appreciate how the actions of a few affected the future of many.

Part One

A ROCK AND A HARD PLACE

My Lord, how full of sweet content,
I pass my years in banishment
Where'er I dwell, I dwell with Thee
In heaven, on earth, or on the sea
Jeanne Marie Boavier de la Motte 1648-1717

CHAPTER ONE

IVAN REMEMBERS

TO THE GULLS WHEELING HIGH ABOVE, THE SHIP IS JUST A silhouette on the trackless ocean. To the short-for-his age, dark-eyed boy standing at the rail, holding tight to its slippery surface it is a moving edifice of noise and bustle, overwhelming with the babble of unfamiliar languages and strange appearances. He is focused on the churning furrows of water rushing by him and ignored by the other third-class passengers on the deck when he wanders through the doors marked, "No admittance. Crew only."

The label pinned to his coat says, Hans Lentz Cabin 69. After three days aboard the ship, the label is bent and twisted. No one ever looks at it anyway, giving him the opportunity to find his way to the second-class deck, which has plenty of spaces for a skinny twelve-year old to hide. Through a gap in the rigging, he can watch the passengers wandering by. He can tell by the ladies' lacy feathered head gear and fancy dresses they must be very rich, which makes him wonder where they are going, and if he will see them in his new home in Canada.

He is glad when the people wander away and leave the deck empty and quiet, surrounded only by ocean and sky. He watches the clouds sailing by and is surprised they look just like the clouds at his old home on the rolling steppes of Southern Russia, near the Sea of Azov, in the part called Ukraine. He remembers the skies with long gossamer threads of white, like spun sugar, and bloated puff balls of mushroom gray or luminous white, and some with no clouds at all. He hears the surging wash of the ocean as the liner forges its way across the turbulent Atlantic, taking him far away from the village he had begun to think of as home. The home he was born in and the faces of his parents have begun to blur in his memory.

He knows he was called Ivan then, Ivan Danilenko. Sometimes at night in a dream or a memory he sees the figure of a man with tangled black hair, and dark eyes, who lifts him high up to the sky and whirls him around, shouting "Fly, little Ivan, fly."

He remembers being snuggled on his mother's lap, twirling a tendril of her long hair, letting her tuneless humming lull him to sleep.

He has an image of playing in a field where the grass was so long it tickled his bare thighs and the sun beat down on his shoulders, where he giggled and clapped his hands as his brother Symon and sister Iryna ran back and forth trying to catch a butterfly, its flitting yellow shape always just beyond their reach. Sometimes he's not sure if it's a memory or something he has been told.

What he remembers most clearly is the three of them sitting in a horse-drawn wagon on the way to the orphanage, after seeing their mother for the last time.

Symon is the oldest of the three and has told him and Iryna what he remembers of their parents. Ivan repeats to himself the melodic sound of their names, Sophia and Orest Danilenko. Symon said they had many friends and took their children on picnics and walks on the fields. To Ivan it sounded like a made-up story, so he didn't always pay very close attention. Symon told him of fun-filled days spent playing with his friends until their mother called him in for supper. Ivan often wondered if that was made up as well.

He had a vague memory of their house in a small village not far from the Molotschna River. It was a hard name to remember but Symon said he should practice it. Nelgowka, Nelgowka, Nelgowka which was near a town called Tokmak, Tokmak, like a clock.

Symon said they lived in part of the house owned by the man who worked with their father in the shop full of sewing machines and bolts of cloth. Their part of the house had three rooms, a kitchen, a sitting area where they also slept, and the small back room where their mother washed endless tubs of laundry. Ivan tried to remember something about the house, but the only thing that came to mind was a bed with a tickly wool blanket and the smell of soap on his mother's arms when she tucked him in at night. Even when he was much older the smell of lye soap brought back a vague recollection of a slim figure struggling to peg a heavy item of clothing to a line. The memory always lingered for a moment then slipped away beyond his reach.

Ivan loved to hear Symon tell how their mother played games with them and told them stories. How they all loved the food she made for them, the thick soup brimming with vegetables and bits of meat from a ham bone, baked delicacies called *pirozhki* and cookies in the shape of stars.

Their father worked at a tailor shop; his nimble fingers created elegant clothing for the rich and powerful, clothing his own family would never be able to afford. Ivan imagined how excited Symon must have been when he was allowed to visit the busy shop, watching the whirring wheel of the manually operated sewing machine, following his father's instructions to keep his hands well away from the flashing needle.

Symon told the younger ones how after coming home from work, their father would swing Iryna high up to the ceiling and tease her about squealing like a little pig; how he would bounce Ivan on his knee and sing a horse-riding song. He would sit down at the table and tell their mother what a great cook she was even if the meal was only fried potatoes and dark rye bread. Iryna and Ivan loved hearing how their father rough-housed with his children, playing tag and telling jokes. Ivan was amazed that their father did these things. His own image of his father was darkness—black stringy hair, brown blazing eyes, dark unshaven face, and curt, angry words.

Symon bragged about going to school, learning the confusing Cyrillic alphabet, and listening to the stories the teacher read to her pupils. He was learning his numbers and enjoying the songs and poetry of the Russian people. School was mainly for boys, so Iryna made Symon teach her all the things he learned at school. She was smart and learned everything he did. He was jealous at times, seeing how easily she made the letters he struggled with, and thinking she learned to read the words more quickly than he did.

Iryna told Ivan the things she remembered, but his own memory seemed to have been washed clean by the deluge of hunger and fear that had controlled their lives after their father couldn't work at the tailor shop anymore.

Neither Symon nor Iryna noticed how gradually the portions of food their mother gave them grew smaller, and that the soup contained more vegetables and less meat. They didn't notice how thin she was becoming, how small her own portions were, or how she rarely sang to Ivan anymore.

They didn't notice how quiet their father had become until his quietness turned to rage, and he drove his fist into the splintery wall of the cooking area in their house. The children huddled in the corner and wondered what they had done to make their father so angry. He shouted and stormed out of the house and didn't come back for a long time.

January 1919

One day their father came home wearing a strange uniform with a red star shape on the sleeve. He told them he had been conscripted into the army, and where their mother should go to collect the money she would be getting every month. She nodded while the tears ran down her cheeks.

Iryna and Ivan hid in a corner of the room and watched while their parents said their goodbyes. Symon stood straight and tall when his father shook hands with him and reminded him, he was now the man of the house. His father's face was stern and tight-lipped, but for a moment wetness shone on the darkly stubbled cheeks. After one last long embrace with their mother, he was gone.

They waited for him to come home, even though their mother told them it might be many months before they would see him again.

Their mother did what she could to keep her family fed after their father left. She tried to collect the money their father had said she would get, but after standing in line with many other women they were told to come back another day, as it had run out. One day she got a few rubles, enough to buy some flour, eggs and milk, and also some used clothing, mostly for Symon who had grown out of everything. After that she never got any more money. When he was older, Ivan realized his family had been caught between the rock of a world war and the hard-place of a revolution.

Their mother tried to explain to the children why she had to work so hard and was often away from home. Taking in washing and cleaning rich people's houses helped pay the rent, but there was not always enough money to buy food for everyone. Twice a week she walked the seven kilometers from their village to Tokmak to clean the government buildings and to bring food for the three hungry children waiting at home. Instead of going to school, Symon began to sneak into backyards, stores and gardens to steal something to sell for a few kopeks, so he could buy one or two buns, an apple or a few potatoes.

Symon never told Ivan until much later that he took his little brother with him when they begged for food, hoping Ivan's sad brown eyes, shaved head and unkempt clothing would encourage passers-by to part with a coin or a bit of food.

The children could only guess how hard their mother worked, but nothing could hide the scarcity of their food or the fact that she was rarely there when they came home from school. Iryna was beyond excited when she was finally allowed to go to school, but she missed many days because her mother was away so often, and no one seemed to care. Schooling was more important for boys.

When Ivan started Kindergarten, Iryna took on the double role of mother and big sister, helping him get ready and making sure Symon didn't just wander the streets with his friends looking for food or money instead of going to school. She took on the job of cleaning and tried to help her mother with the washing but hauling water buckets or hanging heavy wet clothes was beyond her strength. She protected Ivan from bullies and from strangers who had been known to steal children away.

She learned to cook the simple meals they depended on, soup, noodles, potatoes, eggs when they were available, and bread with lard. When mother came home from Tokmak she might bring a special treat–cheese, a few apples or plums.

The thought of food woke them in the morning, followed them to school and waited for them when they opened the door at night. It hung over them like a shadow and blocked out the sun. It didn't leave them after consuming the supper their mother had managed to provide for them. Would there be any food waiting for them in the morning?

CHAPTER TWO

THE EMPTY ROAD

FALL 1919 THEN CAME THE DAY IVAN ONLY VAGUELY REMEM-bered, but about which his brother and sister sobbed in their sleep. They waited for their mother to come home from work and couldn't imagine why she was so late. Mother always brought something for their supper, often just a piece of bread, a sausage if they were lucky, or a few turnips or carrots that could be cooked and help fill empty bellies for a brief time. When darkness set in and she still hadn't come, Symon began to fear something very bad had happened. Ivan and Iryna ran from one window to the other hoping to catch a glimpse of her, but they never did.

As the hours passed Symon's fear turned to anger and his clenched fists pounded the table. His face took on the thunder-cloud look of their father. "Stupid woman," he shouted. "Where is she? She knows we need food."

Iryna shuddered to hear the fury in her brother's voice. It brought back the times when their father took out his worry for the future on his wife or the children. Iryna searched through the cupboards hoping to find something to eat. She found a few tiny potatoes in the vegetable bin and boiled them for their supper.

At bedtime, their mother still wasn't there to tuck them in or kiss them good-night. Ivan cried out his loneliness and his hunger, while Symon sat mutely at the window where he could see the path she would be taking. More and more he was taking on the look of their father, tightened lips and furrowed brows and more scowls than smiles. Iryna often felt the threat of tears but bit her lips and tried to do the jobs her mother would have done.

Morning brought fresh torrents of tears from Ivan and even from Iryna, who could no longer suppress the fear and sadness which overwhelmed her. Symon had no smiles or kind words for his brother and sister, not even a caring look when he told them he had to go out to find some food.

Ivan clung to his brother to keep him from leaving, but Symon pushed him aside and left the house, slamming the door behind him. Ivan sat on the floor, rocking back and forth, tears, dirt and mucous vying for a spot on his face. After a time, he sat motionless, his face convulsing occasionally with a fresh outburst of tears.

Though Iryna shouted at Symon in anger at his long absence, she was relieved when he finally returned. He said nothing and barely glanced at Iryna and Ivan as he threw a packet of food on the table. They scrambled to share the precious hoard, a small sausage, several apples and pieces of bread. They were concentrating on the food and paid little attention when, from the other room, came the splash of water. They thought Symon must be washing up before eating, but when he came out, he didn't eat anything. All afternoon he barely spoke and sat staring out the window. At supper time, he left all the precious bits of meat and bread for Ivan and Iryna. They never wondered why, they just savoured every crumb and relished the ambrosia taste of the apple, right down to the core.

Not an hour passed without Ivan and Iryna waiting and watching for their mother's return. Symon continued his forays into the town and always brought back something to eat. One morning. he brought a square of paper-wrapped chocolate. He cut the chocolate into five small pieces and gave each of them two pieces and kept one for himself. The intoxicating sweetness melted on their tongues and they took tiny nibbles making the delicious treat last as long as possible. Iryna saved one of the two pieces for later. Ivan couldn't resist finishing both of his and then eyeing the piece Iryna was saving. Again, from the washroom came the sound of Symon's hand washing.

Hunger became a living creature that gnawed at their bellies and haunted their dreams with visions of freshly baked bread, steaming bowls of soup and plates of noodles. Iryna and Ivan put all their hopes in Symon, counting on him to bring home some small item of food. They didn't know where he got it, or what he had to do to get it. They just knew he didn't smile much anymore and hardly spoke to them. The only sounds in the house were those of their own weeping.

After almost three weeks of hoping and praying and managing without their mother, the tailor who had worked with their father came to the house to tell them they couldn't live there anymore. Shame was written on his face as he told the children they would have to leave if they couldn't pay the rent that was owing. "If I don't get paid, then I can't pay my bills and I will end up in jail," he said.

Ivan heard the words but understood nothing. Symon knew a little bit about jails. Jails consumed people, turned them into frail shadows of themselves, chewed them up and spat them out like remains of a mouse eaten by a cat.

They took what few possessions they could carry: some clothes, by now filthy and torn, and a picture of their parents taken at their wedding. Ivan brought his prized possession, a tiny, red and black truck his father had been given by a patron of the tailor shop. With it tucked safely into his bag, he was ready to go. They were bewildered and sad as they left the only home they had ever known.

Symon promised to find the children something to eat and told them to hide in the neighbour's cow shed until he came back. The small building was dark, dilapidated and stank of animal manure. Ivan wrinkled his nose in disgust and made a dash for the door. Iryna managed to hold him back and tried to lighten the mood by singing a song their mother had taught them, but soon they huddled together, sobbing miserably.

The milk cow eyed the children suspiciously and went back to chewing her cud. Two piglets snuffled in a tiny pen, and a cat startled them by darting out of a corner and out an opening in the wall. Iryna found a pile of dry straw and drew Ivan down beside her, rocking him as their mother used to do until the motion calmed them both. The darkening barn kept them huddled in the same spot until Symon arrived and handed them each a piece of hard bread and a few bits of crumbly cheese. It was a feast, and as before, neither one of them thought to ask how he had managed to get it. Symon said he wished they could at least wash their hands, but there was no water in the small shed.

Exhausted as they all were, they slept until being woken in the morning by the shuffling sounds of the animals waiting for the farmer coming to feed them. Their neighbour, Vasily, expecting to see only his hungry piglets and the cow waiting to be milked, dropped his empty bucket in shock as three straw-covered figures materialized out of the pile of cattle fodder. "You almost scared me to death! What are you doing here?"

Symon was the spokesman and his lower lip trembled as he relayed the message from the tailor. "We can't live in our house anymore. We can't pay the rent if mother doesn't come back."

Vasily picked the fallen bucket from the floor and shook the straw from its bottom. The frown on his face looked more hopeless than angry. "Well, you can't live here. I'm sorry your mother is missing, but . . . " He shook his head and turned as if to leave the barn. The children, in panic-stricken silence, waited to be ordered out of the building, but instead he motioned for them to follow him into the house.

His wife, Marya, threw him a shocked look when she saw the three disheveled, less than sweet-smelling breakfast guests. His comment was too quiet for the children to hear, but Marya's expression held the same tight-lipped frown as her husband's.

Without a word, she motioned for the children to clean up as well as they could and sit down at the table. She cut three slices of bread, which she handed them along with three very tiny pieces of cheese and a glass of milk each. They devoured the food that was given them and looked for more.

Instead of giving them more food, Marya sat down at the table and took Ivan's hand. "This is all I can give you. You can't stay here. There is only one place you can stay till your mother comes home. The nuns have a building in Tokmak where you can live until she comes back. When she does, I'll tell her where you are."

Symon almost knocked the empty milk glass over as he jumped up from the table and stood as tall and menacing as his slight frame would allow. "It's the orphanage! We are not going to the orphanage. When she comes back, she won't know where we are." Ivan and Iryna had never heard this tone of voice from Symon before. This was more than anger, this was rage and aggression.

"Symon, I promise you I will tell your mother where you are when she comes back." Marya's voice was unyielding. "Vasily will take you now."

Ivan watched in astonishment as Symon snatched up their belongings and shouted at Marya, "We will never go to an orphanage. My mother said those places are hell holes. She would never have let us go to one."

Marya stood by, watching Symon drag his little brother out the door and Iryna sensed that although she wanted to help, there was nothing more she could do. Vasily was already making his way back to his abandoned morning chores and Iryna had no choice but to follow Symon as he rushed away from Marya's kitchen, away from Vasily's barn, and further away from the only house they had ever lived in.

Symon dashed out, turning corners, crossing roads, while Ivan and Iryna tried to keep up. No one spoke to them or even gave them a glance. They were just a few of many children, families, young and old people, all looking for food, shelter, comfort.

Aimless wandering through the town sapped their strength and it was only Ivan's plaintive calls, "*Chekay ne mene*. Wait for me!" that forced them to stop.

A willow bush at the edge of town gave them shelter as they huddled under its low-hanging branches. A nearby creek wended its sluggish way around a grassy bend. Iryna made Ivan wash his dusty, tear stained face and scooped up handfuls of water for him to drink. Symon sat stony-faced and mute trying not to let the two see the tears that threatened. Ivan and Iryna slumped in the tall grass around the trees, restless and bewildered, but trying not to disturb Symon's attempt to sleep.

Finally, Ivan could wait no more and tugged on his brother's jacket demanding, "I'm still hungry."

His little brother's distress brought Symon out of his stupor. "I know, I know. Just give me some time. I'll think of something."

The despondency of the situation left both Ivan and Iryna sitting mutely at the edge of the creek, until Iryna could no longer bear the silence. She remembered her mother's remedy for sadness was to sing, usually Ivan's favorite song, the *Little Hedgehog* song. In a quavering voice she began the tune and soon Ivan joined in. Even Symon's glum face held a small smile when they reached the part about the "prickly, stickily, little hedgehog child".

The song seemed to break the spell. Symon got to his feet and without a word began the walk back to the village. Iryna and Ivan were not about to be left behind and followed their brother as he wandered up one street and down another. Ivan watched as he walked casually by a street merchant and managed to steal two small apples, which they shared. Later in the day a scrawny old woman, listlessly packing up her goods for the night, gave them a few crumbly hard crusts from a loaf of rye bread. It was almost dark when they snuck back into Vasily's cow barn. His evening milking was done so they were safe for the night.

Exhaustion won out over hunger and they slept until morning when they awoke to find Vasily standing over them, milking pail in hand. Iryna and Ivan hunkered down in the straw, waiting for angry recriminations from Vasily, while Symon jumped up ready to defend their presence. Vasily looked more resigned than angry and told them to go into the house.

Marya met them at the door as if she had been waiting for them. She helped the children clean up after their night in the barn and let them sit at the table until Vasily came in.

She gave Iryna a small cloth-wrapped package, "This is all I can give you. We have nothing more to spare."

"You have to go to the orphanage," Vasily's face was expression-less and his voice was stern. "They will give you food. This is all we can give you." He handed Iryna three small pieces of cheese to add to the packet of bread. "I will take you to the orphanage now. You will die on the streets if you don't go. Look at your little brother. He needs food now, and a place to sleep."

Symon's dark eyes blazed with fury. "We are not going!"

His shouts were silenced as Vasily seized the boy and rushed him out to the waiting horse-drawn cart. There was no choice. Iryna and Ivan wailed with fear but followed Vasily and were lifted up into the cart. As it began to move, Iryna turned to catch one last glimpse of the thatched-roof house beside Vasily and Marya's, the house they called home. The only spot of colour relieving the greyness of its surroundings was the red and yellow apron Marya used to wipe her eyes as she watched them go.

The bread and cheese lasted only for a small part of the journey.

CHAPTER THREE

THE NUN'S ORPHANAGE

October 1919

THE ORPHANAGE WAS A DARK BRICK STRUCTURE, COLD AND uninviting. A stone fence surrounded the gray walls, interrupted by a once-majestic, pillared gate and a few bare trees. Dry grass rustled as a brisk fall wind lifted dead leaves and sent them whirling to the roof top. Several children sat on a bench near the gate, playing with some objects they tossed at each other. Inside the fence two boys were wrestling on the ground, encouraged by shouts from children watching.

Vasily lifted Ivan and Iryna from the cart and Symon had no choice but to follow. "Go through the gate," he instructed them. "Then through the door at the side of the building. Tell the nun Vasily sent you."

Without another word, Vasily climbed onto his cart and was gone before the bewildered siblings had a chance to react.

The children in the yard stopped playing and stared at the newcomers. "Look, here come some more scared rabbits looking for food. *Ydy het*!" they shouted. "Go away!"

Ivan was glad when Symon straightened himself to full height and shouted back. "I don't have to. I'm coming to see the nun. Vasily knows her."

By now they had reached the side door which opened before they had a chance to knock. An elderly nun dressed in black, turned a frowning face on the children.

Symon's voice sounded loud and resolute. "Vasily said to tell you he sent us here."

"Oh, not more of Vasily's kids." muttered the nun as she turned and led them into the building. The room they found themselves in was dark and crowded with trestle tables and backless benches. If its look was uninviting, its smell was even less so.

Ivan pulled on Iryna's hand turning back the way they had come. "It stinks, I don't like it here."

The nun gave them all an annoyed glance, "Wait till it's full of filthy children. You'll think this smells like roses. You two, come with me. I'll find some place for you. You, girl, go with Berta", she said pointing to a scruffy young girl with straggly, matted black hair and a filthy apron over a tattered dress.

The girl's dark eyes glittered and something which passed for a smile showed blackened gaps in yellowed teeth. Iryna did as she was told, watching as her brothers went off with the nun, and a feeling of dread replaced the ravenous hunger for food.

Berta giggled and grabbed Iryna's hand. Iryna thought nothing seemed even remotely funny. "You look pretty," whispered Berta and Iryna smelled the fetid odor of her breathe as she leaned uncomfortably close. "You can have the bed next to mine. I save it for the pretty ones."

Iryna shivered in the growing chill as they progressed down a long dark hallway. Doors opened to other rooms, some with ragged, unmade shelf-like beds, some with girls huddled under ragtag sheets and articles of clothing. The occupants of the beds showed very little interest in the newcomer. Even from a distance Iryna could see their vacant expressions. No sound came from them except the odd muffled moan or sniffle. Iryna wanted only to escape. Would she ever see Symon or Ivan again?

At the far end of the hallway, Berta grinned as she showed the girl another room. The beds in this room had a pillow, a few blankets and were made up to look inviting. Iryna wanted nothing more than to pull a blanket over her head and disappear into the depths of unconsciousness.

From a distance came the sound of a screaming child, its wails reaching a high-pitched, cry of pain and fear. Iryna covered her ears to shut out the sound. Could it be Ivan? The thought sent her on a dash for the doorway, back in the direction they had come, back to Ivan, to Symon, back to the door which led away from this place. Berta had anticipated the move before it had even occurred to Iryna, and was blocking the doorway, her face contorted with that gap-toothed grin that seemed more evil than funny.

"That's my brother," shouted Iryna, "I have to go to him. Get out of the way! Let me out!"

"Don't worry, someone will take care of him. He will be fine. Come I will show you your bed," Berta's mocking smile belied her words. "See, he stopped already. You will see him at supper time."

Before Iryna had time to react, she had been pushed onto a bed and Berta had forced her to swing her trembling legs under the tattered coverlet. Berta's grin gave Iryna the shivers, though the girl spoke less roughly. "Here, you scared little mouse, have a rest. I'll be back later."

Berta left the room and closed the door behind her. That was when Iryna noticed that one of the other beds was occupied. She saw a pair of huge dark eyes staring at her from under a mat of tousled hair. A girl about her own age lay huddled under a ragged blanket; her face was dark with dirt except for rivulets of tears that had washed a path down her cheeks.

The girl shook uncontrollably, making the words she spoke almost inaudible, and Iryna heard only, "Don't let her touch me. She's mean! Don't let her get near you. She will hurt you bad."

Iryna hunched down on the hard, uninviting cot, curling herself around the only thing left of her other life, the small bag of clothes she had brought with her, a dress, a sweater her mother had made, a pair of underwear, two mismatched stockings and a blue hair-bow worn only once. She covered her head and squeezed her eyes shut, every muscle in her body clenched in a knot until exhaustion overtook her and her body relaxed into exhausted sleep.

CHAPTER FOUR

A BOWL OF LUMPY PORRIDGE

SYMON AND IVAN WERE LED DOWN A DARK HALLWAY OPENING to other rooms with mattress-covered floors and shelf-like bunks holding odd bits of blankets or clothing. Many of the beds were empty, but some were occupied by thin, unkempt boys, huddled together for warmth or protection. The nun told Symon that his brother would have to sleep in the children's section where he would be better looked after.

Ivan's screams filled the hallway when he realized he was about to be separated from his brother. Symon had never heard such shrieks of fear from him. "I'll look after him," he told the nun as the noise of his brother's wailing brought shouts of indignation from the other children in the room.

The nun gave in and shoved the trembling child into Symon's hands. "See that you do. I don't need another screaming brat causing trouble. You'll be the one screaming if you don't keep him quiet."

Ivan clung to Symon with a death grip as the nun showed them to a straw-filled sack covering rough planks. "You'll have to share the bed if your brother won't go to the kid's corner."

"Where is my sister? I want to see my sister!" demanded Symon.

"You can see her at supper time." He felt guilty that his joy at the nun's mention of food overrode his relief at the prospect of seeing Iryna again. Both boys sat on the narrow bed, clutching their bags of clothing.

Symon looked at the many thin, ragged children, wandering aimlessly around the room or huddled on their beds wrapped in the few bed-clothes they owned. One small boy hugged a furry, brown stuffed bear with one beady eye, and a leg hanging by a thread. A bigger boy, wearing nothing but a thin night shirt and a tattered wool hat, kept making moves to steal the toy, causing the boy to hug his bear with a possessiveness bordering on panic. A shout from across the room caused the would-be thief to slink away and throw himself onto a bare mattress where he covered his head with a dirty, grey pillow. Symon turned his head away, embarrassed at the sight of the boy's bare buttocks.

Another nun had come into the room, younger, friendlier but with a determined look in her eyes as she headed toward the boys. "I'm Sister Elizaveta, come with me. It's time for a louse check." Ivan was already being led away and Symon followed; anywhere was better than here.

The room they entered resembled a clinic or hospital room, with a small table, a chair and a cot. Indignity followed indignity as the nun forced them to strip to their underwear and examined both their bodies and the clothing. "You are fortunate," she said, "You do not have lice . . . yet, so come with me."

The larger room to which they were led was more cheerful, with beds made-up with clean bedding and even some with pillows. Boys of all ages sat or lay on their beds, some deathly quiet, heads buried in the sparse bedding, others livelier, even rowdy as they shouted to each other across the room. Symon thought of a boarding school he had once been in, where boys from out of the village lived while attending the local school. It gave him hope, maybe the orphanage wasn't as bad as he had expected.

The beds were meant for one child, but two skinny bodies fit with room to spare. Exhaustion had taken a toll on the two and each slept for short periods of time. When Ivan awoke, he saw Symon sitting on one of the beds near three other boys. They seemed friendly enough, and he heard Symon laughing at something they said to him.

Ivan's eyelids drooped, and he soon drifted off to sleep again to be woken by Symon saying, "Come on, it's supper time. We will see Iryna."

They were taken to a smaller room, a room with pans for washing hands and faces, then to the room with the trestle tables. Many children were already seated, concentrating on eating the food in their bowls. No one questioned what they were given, it was food– soup with a few vegetables and a generous slice of bread.

Both Symon and Ivan were absorbed by the pleasure of eating before they noticed Iryna sitting at a table with some other girls, focused on spooning the food into her mouth. In their joy at seeing each other again, everything else was momentarily forgotten. Ivan forgot the rule about staying in the boys' section and rushed over to hug her, giving Symon an excuse to greet her as well. He ruffled her hair and pulled a stalk of straw from a tangled braid. Iryna held on to her brothers with a ferocious grip that was released only when Sister Elizaveta came to warn them to stay at their assigned table.

Symon threw an embarrassed look at her before hurrying his little brother back to his place. Ivan waited for a rebuke from his brother for breaking the rules but was relieved that Symon's hand on his shoulder was gentle and light.

Back at his place, Symon even smiled at the boy seated next to him, who in return shared valuable information with him.

"It's lucky you don't have lice. Stay as far away from anyone who looks dirty. Check your clothes and wash whenever you can. You'll be able to stay in this part of the building as long as you don't have lice. Keep a look-out tomorrow when we go out in the yard. You will probably be able talk to your sister."

The siblings knew very little about lice. They were soon informed that lice carried the dreaded typhus, a disease that could kill you. In the orphanage, children who were infested with lice often huddled naked on their shelf beds, stripped of the clothing which harboured the creatures. Washing did not get rid of them. There was no other option but to burn the clothing, leaving children with nothing.

Simon, Iryna and Ivan's first few days at the orphanage passed in a blur of confusion. The day the boys were united with Iryna brought them all comfort and assurance. The play yard seemed to hold fewer children than usual, and Symon gave a shout of recognition as he spotted his sister standing in a sheltered corner.

Great sobs wracked Iryna's body as she was enveloped in a hug from her brothers. Her voice was high-pitched and shaky as she pleaded with her brothers. "I want to be with you. I don't like it here. Berta is mean and nasty. She steals our food and tries to get in our beds."

Ivan seemed not to hear Iryna's complaints and buried his face in her chest and rocked back and forth, as he hugged his sister close.

"Who is this?" asked Symon, noticing a smaller, frightened-looking child huddled close to his sister.

"This is Wilimina. She sleeps in the room I'm in. She is afraid of Berta too. Girls who don't have lice sleep in Berta's room. I was afraid I would never see you again!" Iryna squared her shoulders and tightened her hold on her little brother.

Symon could tell she was trying hard to sound brave.

Symon tried to help his sister understand how important it was to stay louse-free, but Iryna only wanted to be near her brothers and seemed oblivious to any other danger.

Symon was not used to comforting his younger siblings; that had always been their mother's task. "You have to be brave," he counselled, "Meet us here whenever you are outside. Don't worry. You will be fine."

Iryna nodded and watched her brothers find other activities to keep them occupied. Symon turned back to wave at the forlorn little figure and felt sorry he didn't know how to make her feel better.

Empty days followed nights filled with the sobs, moans, and terrifying shrieks of crying children. For a while, the three siblings, especially Iryna, looked for ways to escape. Yet, in spite of its faults, the orphanage offered powerful compensations: a breakfast bowl of lumpy porridge, a supper bowl of bits of chicken and a helping of noodles, a slice of bread, a dried apple or plum. The food brought colour to small cheeks, and gradually even Iryna felt her spirits lifting.

Their days began to develop a pattern. Symon spent his time with three other boys playing with a ball they had found or huddled in a corner sharing a cigar smuggled in through a break in the fence. Ivan was convinced to stay in the little kid's room during the day, where Sister Sophia tried to play games with the younger ones and encouraged them to listen to stories or sing songs.

Ivan's fifth birthday came and went without celebration, remembered only because Iryna still had some recollection of special days. She knew Ivan's birthday came at the beginning of winter, and when she told him he was five years old, he celebrated by bringing out the toy truck from his bag of clothes and played with it under his ragged blanket. He polished the faded black and red surface and checked the wheels to make sure they still turned. He drove the tiny roofless vehicle up pillow mountains and along blanket roads, then placed it back in its hiding place.

An object as rare as the toy truck had to be kept well hidden from anyone on the look-out for merchandise to sell. Ivan had been strongly warned by Symon of the need for secrecy. He did what Symon told him and gave little thought to anything but spending his nights near his brother and looking forward to his daily ration of food.

Winter chill kept them indoors most of the time, and the dark eating area smelled less and less like roses every day. Morning playtime brought a smile to Iryna's face when she spotted one or both of her brothers. Because they had no warm clothing, the three siblings were constantly on the look-out for unused or discarded bits of clothing or blankets to cover themselves, while they waited for their morning meeting times.

Wilimina and several other girls played games using odds and ends found in the yard, or dolls fashioned from bits of cloth and string, and for want of anything else to do, Iryna joined in.

Sister Sophia tried to help the school age children with a modicum of education, though the scarcity of materials made it difficult. The few pencils and notebooks had to be shared between all the children. Sister Sophia soon saw Iryna's potential for learning and made sure she had use of a pencil and notebook more often.

Iryna watched every day as people came and went through the side doors, waiting for a sign of Vasily or Marya coming to tell them their mother had returned. Her heart raced the day she saw a horse and cart making its way down the road, and yes, it was stopping! The man who stepped down from the cart looked bent and worn-out, his farm clothing muddy and patched. Though she could only see the back of his body, she was sure it was Vasily.

Ignoring the shouts from Sister Sophia, she ran from the classroom ready to welcome her long-awaited neighbour. "Vasily, it's me, Iryna! I've been waiting so long! Is my mother back?" Couldn't he hear her? Why didn't he stop? "Vasily, it's me! Stop, stop!"

When she reached him, she tugged at his jacket, waiting for a sign of recognition. The man she saw was swarthy and unshaven, just like Vasily, his face aloof and serious like Vasily's, but it wasn't him. She felt weak with disappointment and her knees folded under her. The splintery boards of the floor stabbed at her cheek while her tears mixed with the muddy boot prints of the man who brought a bag of potatoes every now and then. Sister Sophia lifted her to her feet, and for the moment, her strong arms felt gentle and comforting.

Never again would she let herself hope for something that was hopeless, watching the door or the window hoping an approaching figure was someone she knew. Still, her heart skipped a beat at the sight of a red and yellow apron worn by an orphanage worker. The man from the tailor shop, bringing scraps of cloth for the nuns to sew into blankets, sent her hopes soaring for a brief moment. Each disappointment threw her into a darkness of despair, relieved only by the playground visits with Symon and Ivan.

While Symon dreamed of getting a job at the tailor shop like his father, making enough money to rent back their old house and to send his siblings to school, Ivan thought only of having enough to eat and seeing his brother and sister every day.

The children in the louse-free rooms, known as the clean rooms, were examined every day for any sign of the dreaded pests. Louse infestation meant being separated from the others. Iryna became paranoid at the smallest sign of bites or itchiness. She and Wilimina examined each other's hair and clothing every day.

The chill and darkness of winter finally passed, and the mild spring sunlight filled their rooms. The children in the clean rooms no longer needed to huddle together for warmth. They spread their arms and legs to capture the balminess and ran around the yard like spring colts. The nuns smiled more, and hope began to blossom. The food took on colour; a red radish or a leaf of green lettuce, a soup bowl with bits of green floating among the brown of last year's potato or turnip.

CHAPTER FIVE

FOOD, FOOD, FOOD

July 1920

THE GOOD DAYS WERE NOT TO LAST. THOUGH THE HEAT OF summer spread through the rooms, the atmosphere grew chillier. One morning, some of the nuns, the kinder, gentler ones, were gone.

Ivan, waiting for Sister Sophia, clung to his bag of clothes and sobbed into his pillow when she didn't come. The children searched for her, asked when she would be back, but no one knew. The nuns who had stayed had nothing but curt answers for the children. When they asked for more porridge or soup or bread, they were told there was no more. The cheeks that had grown rosier faded to white and hunger took up residence in the home once more. Sister Lilya, Sister Manya and Sister Elizaveta left one evening, and though the children waited for them, they never came back.

A word was heard, an unfamiliar word, a Russian word, an ugly word. *Bolshevik.* The Catholics were out, the Bolsheviks were in. The next morning, new workers, Luba, Vanya and Boras had taken the place of the nuns. They tried to look after the children, but there were so many and so few workers, so many hungry mouths and so little food.

Not as many louse checks were done. The older children took on the job and did the best they could at keeping the clean rooms free of the tiny marauders. Symon and Ivan and some of the other boys swept the rooms and hung the clothes and blankets outside to shake out the accumulating dirt and debris. Iryna and Wilimina followed their example and tried to keep up a standard of cleanliness, but it was a losing battle. The siblings spent more time together as none of the workers seemed to care where they went, or with whom. They all came back at mealtimes.

Food, food, food. They dreamed of it, they talked of it, they longed for it, they waited for it. There was never enough. Hunger roamed the halls like an errant peddler dispensing a bounty of sickness, sadness, despair and death.

Symon and two of his friends made their way out of the yard through a break in the fence and wandered the streets along with other children. They looked for businesses that were still open, hoping to find discarded goods or bits of food or saleable items. Some businesses were boarded up, but others seemed to carry on in a limited way. The boys tried to enter the boarded-up ones in their search for items to sell. They soon learned that others had got there before them and meeting a hungry, angry individual in a darkened building was not to be desired. Instead, they learned to check refuse bins and empty containers for the odd item to use or sell.

Symon relearned the art of thievery, and never came back without bits of food to share with Iryna, Ivan, and others. He learned from children on the street the best places to beg for food. He and two of his friends brought back items of clothing: stockings, underwear, shirts and trousers. No one knew how the three were able to lay their hands on the rare and valuable goods. Ivan and Iryna and others were the beneficiaries of their largess; a small black market thrived and for a time the resourceful group held their own.

September 1920

The warm days couldn't last forever. As fall drew near, food became scarcer as did ways of finding it. As winter stretched before them, other, more unsavoury ways of earning money were all that was left to them. Stealing food or possessions became more difficult, as everyone guarded their belongings with a passion. What was left? Committing acts of crime, in partnership with older, more experienced law-breakers.

Ivan was happy his brother's forays into town became fewer and farther between, but Symon knew without them they would not survive the winter. He also knew their venturing couldn't last. They knew the jig was up the evening he and two others snuck back through the hole in the fence to find the orphanage worker Boris, waiting for them.

"So, my little thieves, where did you find these goodies?" His hand tightened on Symon's arm till the pain brought an involuntary exclamation of protest. "Either you tell me, or I'll make sure the boss hears about it and you will end up with nothing."

"I'll tell you," said Symon, struggling to escape the vice-like grip. "There is a man living by himself in the apartment near the government building. He's lonely. He needs someone to keep him company. We . . . take turns . . . spending time with him, and he gets the stuff for us."

"Aha, you little tramps. Do you . . . you know, do you like spending time with him?"

The boys vehemently denied even the implication. The only good days were when it was someone else's turn. Symon's skin crawled when he had to keep the man company, but the joy on his sister and brother's faces when he gave them the food made it worthwhile.

"We don't like it, but we're hungry. What should we do?"

Boris grinned and let go of Symon's arm. "Well, we can make a deal here. You give me half the stuff you get, and I'll keep my mouth shut. You understand?"

Symon nodded. His friends, Milos and Yanove stood mutely by, their eyes filling with misery, as they knew what was being asked of them.

The rations provided by the orphanage decreased as Symon and his friends found less and less food and fewer goods to trade.

The children occupied their beds for longer periods of time as energy waned and hope diminished.

CHAPTER SIX

WHERE IS IRYNA?

December 1920

ONE DAY IRYNA DID NOT COME INTO THE YARD TO MEET HER brothers. When three days had passed without a sign of her, Ivan became obsessed with wanting to know where she was, and Symon grew frantic with worry. Finally, he confronted Luba, the girls' worker, and what he heard caused an icy lump to form in his belly.

"She is not feeling well. When she feels better you will be able to see her."

The next day Luba told them Iryna had been moved to the infirmary where she would get better care. The news brought some comfort. Surely, she would get better food and would soon be well.

After two days of waiting, Luba came to tell them the news that was to change their lives forever. "We are sorry to tell you, your sister died last night. We did everything we could, but we couldn't save her."

Luba looked genuinely sympathetic and hugged Ivan whose face was frozen in shock. Symon stared mutely at her as if he had not understood a word she said. *Died? Not Iryna, his beautiful dark-eyed little sister who smiled even when she was hungry, who shared her food with her little brother when she had almost nothing to give! It couldn't be true!* Every part of his body screamed *No! No!* even though not a sound escaped his lips.

"There will be a funeral for your sister tomorrow." said Luba, "I will come for you."

As if in a trance, the two boys followed Luba back to their room. Then Ivan's small face crumpled, and his anguished wails caught the attention of every child in the crowded room.

"Where is Iryna? I want to see Iryna."

Symon still could not believe what he had heard and had no words to comfort his brother. They huddled on their narrow bed, struck dumb by the devastating news, the silence broken only by outbursts of Ivan's weeping. Symon's limited experience with his Russian Orthodox upbringing gave him a smattering of knowledge of what occurred at a funeral. He knew it had something to do with a priest. No such person came. No one came to give them support, to explain what had happened, to hold their hands or to dry their tears. The only comfort they received came at supper time by way of a fuller bowl of watery soup.

In the darkness of the night they clung to each other until finally Ivan's body relaxed into sleep. Symon held back his tears and swallowed the lump in his throat, but the pain that filled his chest threatened to overwhelm him. He had heard people say their hearts were breaking and he wondered if this was how it felt.

Luba came the next morning and they walked the short distance to a fence-enclosed field where a horse-drawn cart stood near a mound of freshly dug soil. Other children joined the group and stood staring mutely at the dark bundled shapes lying side-by-side in the back of the cart. The stillness was broken only by the jingling rattle of the horse's harness and the creak of the cart as the bundles were removed. One by one they were placed in their final resting place.

Like a requiem for a lost child, came Ivan's keening lament, "Where is Iryna? Why can't I see Iryna?"

As if in commiseration, clouds drifted over the sun and the wind arose. Ivan's body gave a jolt at every thudding sound of earth being thrown into the open pit. Symon held tight to his little brother's hand and when the empty cart moved away from the mounded soil, he reached a decision. It was time to leave this place, or Ivan's body would be the next bundle in the cart.

In the quiet of the winter nights that followed, he lay awake remembering Iryna, how she smiled, how she sang and how she tended to her brothers. He remembered and he planned. To the small hoard of the only things he owned, Symon began to add items he thought might be useful on their journey home: dried bits of fruit or meat, hard chunks of rye bread, anything edible that could last. From Iryna's bag he took any item of clothing that could help keep him or Ivan warm. Why he kept Iryna's blue hair-bow, which her worker gave him the day of the funeral, he didn't know. Ivan's memories faded, and he knew only that he would never see his sister again.

March 1921

Spring came early in the southern region of Ukraine. When the buds on the spreading oak tree in the orphanage yard began to swell with a tinge of green, Symon decided it was time to go. There was only one place to go–home, the only home they knew, the house they lived in during the good years with their mother and father, the three-roomed part of the tailor's house in the village of Nolgowka, next door to Marya and Vasily.

Vasily's horse-drawn cart had covered the distance between their home and the orphanage in only a few hours. By foot, the journey seemed endless. Symon thought he knew the right direction, but as they left the town behind everything began to look so strange. Had they been on this road before?

They were caught up in the melee of roaming children, all searching for something, for food, for shelter, for anything that would give them comfort in the middle of a storm of need. How frail most of them looked, how thin, how pale, how dangerous. The little hoard of food Symon had managed to collect had to be consumed out of sight, under a bridge, behind an empty building; anywhere they were less likely to be seen.

Symon soon lost any sense of where they should be heading, wandering aimlessly, anywhere to escape the hordes of the hungry. Ivan followed robotically, empty eyed.

They had been walking on and off for three days, stopping here and there, finding something to eat, seeking out shelter or a place to sleep. Ivan's steps stumbled and became slower. They had to find a place to rest, a place where there was food.

Symon seemed to have an instinct for finding someone who was willing to feed two hungry boys in return for some small job. He was doing his best, but he could see Ivan's health was fading. His steps shortened, and he fell asleep at every rest stop. His eyes seemed to sink farther into the waxen skull. He rarely smiled, even at the antics of a small dog that followed them for a short distance.

They found shelter under the low-hanging branches of some early budding willows, where the long grass had been flattened by another resting creature. For now, it was the end of the road. In a rare show of affection, Symon pulled his brother close, whispering his mother's good night mantra, "See you in the morning."

Part Two

MOLOTSCHNA MENNONITE COLONY, UKRAINE, SOUTHERN RUSSIA

To me remains nor place nor time;
My country is in every clime;
I can be calm and free from care
On any shore, since God is there.
Jeanne Marie Boavier de la Motte 1648-1717

CHAPTER SEVEN

MOVING PICTURES

1914

THE SMALL SEPIA PHOTO, ON THE BACK WRITTEN, *Tina and Sara, August 1st,* lies almost forgotten in a misshapen metal box covered with foreign-looking words. It has found its way across the steppes of Russia, over the Atlantic Ocean, the Rocky Shield and the flat prairies of Canada, to a small farmhouse in Alberta.

Two girls posed for a birthday photograph that day, in the sunny comfort of Blumenau, the peaceful Mennonite village, part of the Molotschna Colony in Southern Russia. Could anyone ever have known that in another part of the world, the stage was being set for a drama destined to play itself out in acts of brutality, affecting not only its actors, but its entire world audience?

For Tina Boldt and her stepsister, Sara Schroeder, August 1st, 1914 was special only because a photographer was coming all the way from Melitopal to Blumenau to take photographs of anyone who could afford to pay.

Tina's mother, Maria Schroeder, considered a fifteenth birthday a suitable occasion for her daughter's first formal photograph. Tina's stepfather, David Schroeder, did not always agree with his wife, but the two girls knew he could not ignore their pleading, and if they presented a united front, he would agree.

"What will we wear for the picture?" asked Sara, after the question was settled in their favour. "I like my dark blue with the buttons running down the side."

"Yes. Good choice. With one of Mama's white crochet collars? We'll look more like real sisters if we wear the same thing."

"Yes, let's have Aunt Helena put our hair up so we look more grown-up." Sara's enthusiasm sent her dark curls bouncing, and Tina wondered whether her dimple-cheeked sister would ever look grown-up.

The photographer brought his portable back-drop of ornate furniture and a flowery trellis, but in August, in the heat of a South Ukrainian summer, the whole world served as a romantic backdrop: the spreading oak tree, the patch of primroses, the multi-coloured mallow, drooping sunflowers, even the garden bench.

The photography session took longer than expected. The girls were happy when the photographer packed up his equipment and was on his way, with promises he would make every effort to have the pictures ready for viewing on the day of the birthday celebration.

Birthdays meant relatives would come to celebrate. The sturdy brick Schroeder house, surrounded by oak and elm trees, shrubs and summer blossoms, was polished and shiny, ready for the influx. The garden path leading from the back of the long, attached barn and storage shed to the house, had been swept clean of dead leaves and branches, and the flower patch weeded and dead-headed.

"What will people say if our garden path is messy?" It was one of Maria Schroeder's concerns, "What will people say?"

Relatives came not only to celebrate, but also to inspect and evaluate.

The birthday *fesper*, afternoon coffee, would be served with an amazing assortment of sweet rolls and cookies. Maria was not to be outdone by the melt-in-your-mouth flakiness of Tante Lentz's *zucker schnetki*, with or Cousin Lydia's spicy *pfeffernuesse*, or next-door neighbour Mrs. Honey-bee Janzen's sweet tarts.

Everyone, including Tina and Sara, looked forward to seeing aunts, uncles and cousins, catching up on the news of marriages, engagements, new babies and inevitably, the deaths of aging relatives. Advice was given, gossip exchanged, and memories unearthed.

There would be small homemade gifts, handkerchiefs, gloves or scarves in winter, in summer a frilly apron or hair bow. Parents often chose a fifteenth birthday to give their daughter some special memento—an ivory comb, hair clips, jewelry or a carefully crafted linen chest. Both Tina and Sara discovered a pin-on watch at their breakfast plate that morning, silver filigree outlining a dainty face with delicate black hands pointing to tiny numbers. No doubt it had been purchased in Kiev, from the general store owned by David's long-time friend, Efim Golub. It was a rare and unique gift, cherished by the girls until somehow lost in the in the dark nooks and crannies of life.

It was a day for walking in the warm sunshine, relaxing, visiting, playing hide-and-seek or tag in the waving clover and brome grasses of the common meadow. Two of Sara's brothers had little children of their own, so the house was full of noise and laughter. Relatives came to help, so the birthday girls were free for the day.

The day was a huge success. What more could one ask for, than a warm, sunny August day, relatives, friends, tasty food and thoughtful matching gifts? The real excitement, of course, lay in seeing the finished photographs. They had arrived in time for the birthday and been kept packed until the great unveiling. After the afternoon *fesper*, as everyone still sat at the table, Tina unfolded the brown paper package and removed the precious contents. Sara did the same, and with a critical eye each girl studied the only photos ever taken of the two of them together.

The frown on Sara's face told the story. "We both look like we're mad at the world. Is that how I look? I didn't feel mad."

Tina was no happier with the result. "I look like an old lady. We should have asked Auntie to wave our hair a little bit more, but it really was the photographer's fault. He wouldn't let us smile, even a little bit."

Both Maria and David beamed with pride and assured the girls they looked very nice and the photo would be a wonderful remembrance of their fifteenth birthday. The photos were passed around and approval was expressed by everyone. Extravagant praise was not a feature of Mennonite culture.

Sara put her photo back in its package, "Maybe someday our children or grandchildren will look at this picture and wonder why we look so serious."

Tina smiled at the possibility. "Yes, they won't know how hard it was not to laugh when the photographer told us we should stop being silly and act like ladies."

Anyone observing the two girls would never have guessed they had been sisters for only two years, stepsisters if one wanted to be specific. Not that they looked alike, nothing could be further from reality. Tina's fair hair and blue eyes matched her rosy-pink complexion, while Sara's dark curly hair and sparkling brown eyes were complemented by the tawny colour of her skin. Tina was considered the quiet one, while Sara was more confidant and out-going. Sara, being the younger of the two by forty-six days (as she was constantly reminded), tended to be more assertive, or aggressive some people said. "When Sara makes up her mind, look out, don't cross her."

Tina's two younger brothers, Isaac and Cornelius resembled their older sister only in the brilliant blue of their eyes. They were known as the Terrible Twosome, who, being surrounded by girls, felt the need to attract attention any way they could. Little Neta was the baby of the family—everyone's favorite, as smart as her sisters and even prettier.

Tina maintained the best thing that had ever happened in her own life was getting Sara as a stepsister.

For the first eleven years of her life she lived in the small Mennonite village of Blumenau with her parents, Maria and Isaac Boldt, and as time went by, with Isaac, Cornelius and little Neta. No one ever asked if she was happy. Happiness was not everything, but she knew that since Sara had become part of the family, life had become even better.

The Boldt family had visited some of the other sixty villages in the Molotschna Mennonite Colony, but they all agreed Blumenau was the best, with its carefully-tended rows of poplars, oaks, and elm trees, the plum, cherry and apple orchards, the well-kept yards surrounded by gardens and flower beds, the shaded streets and prosperous businesses backed by fertile fields of grain, and steppes of waving grass.

When Tina was eleven, her father, Isaac Boldt, died at the age of fifty-seven after only a few months of illness.

The death of Tina's father came as a shock to the community, probably even more than to his children. In a close-knit place with limited health care, death was not unusual, but the death of a close friend or neighbour was a blow.

The children had grown used to their father's absence on church and community business, knowing that at the end of the week or after a few days, he would be home again. His absence after his death seemed not so different, at first. They watched and participated in the rituals of death in the family and accepted it with the equanimity of the young.

Neighbours brought food, church elders came with words of comfort, and friends came to sit with their mother. Maria, the new widow, seemed to find comfort in relating the circumstances of her husband's sudden death over and over. Her sadness filled the house and conveyed itself to the children.

No one asked Tina or her brothers how they felt about the death of their father. The boys stood by, not knowing any words to say, relieved when they could get out of doors and take up their games. Tina felt guilty wishing she could join them.

Maria explained how her husband had begun feeling weak and tired and needed help getting out of bed in the morning. He coughed so much and was short of breath. The doctor came several times and left some medication, which seemed to help for a while, but overnight his weight began to melt away and he went from being a healthy individual to a pale, shaky old man. Soon he was unable to get out of bed, and Aunt Helena and Uncle Jakob came to help look after him as his condition deteriorated.

All her life, Tina remembered how only a few days after she had come, Aunt Helena called the children to their father's bedside. Her aunt's words became part of the quilt of memories which sustained her through the years.

"Come quickly, children, your father is dying."

Maria was seated by her husband's side, holding his hand and smoothing the sparse hair from his forehead. Tina heard the rattling sound of her father's breathing and thought he must be sleeping. Then his gasping breaths became slower and further apart. Tina held her own breath waiting for her father's next one which never came. Her mother shook her head in disbelief as the tears rolled down her cheeks.

Stillness filled the room, broken only by their Uncle Jacob's words, "He's gone."

The children, distressed by what they didn't understand, held onto each other until their mother pulled them close for a silent good-bye.

Except for two-year-old Neta, who stayed with her mother, the children spent the rest of the evening at their Oma Driedeger's. The boys enjoyed the hot cocoa she made for them, but Tina didn't feel right enjoying her cocoa on such a sad day.

Later, she tried to fix in her mind everything that had happened following their father's death, but all was in chaos and confusion as people came and went through the house. Neighbours brought food and baking for the funeral *fesper* and offered bed and board to visitors. The preachers came with prayers and words of comfort.

Preparations for the funeral were quickly underway. Maria went through the motions, finding meals for the guests, clean clothes for the children, black arm bands for the boys, black hair ribbons for the girls, a black dress for her herself. Her face was expressionless, and Tina wondered how her mother could be so calm. Weren't people supposed to cry when someone died?

Tina was allowed to choose a song for the funeral and to help make the greenery wreaths, tying them with white ribbon on which were stenciled the words "Safe in His arms" and "Home at Last".

At the funeral, sad songs and prayers and the words of comfort from the preacher, finally brought tears to Tina's eyes. The life story of her father was told by his brother, Tina's Uncle Kolya. She learned more about her father from his eulogy than she had ever known about him during his lifetime.

After the final tribute, the coffin was carried to the village cemetery by two close friends, three of her father's Boldt cousins and a church worker.

Tina stood close to her mother as the minister uttered the words of commitment, "In sure and certain hope of the resurrection to eternal life through the Lord Jesus Christ." Then, the last *Auf Wiedersehen,* the words which were spoken with the assurance and hope of another meeting.

She felt Maria's body flinch at the unearthly sound of the earth thrown onto the wooden coffin. Tina was glad when it was over and her mother's hold on her arm relaxed.

The green wreaths were placed on the earthen mound, their words of comfort fluttering in the breeze. Maria and the children stood for a few minutes more after the others had left. Little Neta picked up a fallen branch of greenery and threw it with baby exuberance onto the pile of wreaths. Isaac and Cornelius tried to suppress the smiles they knew were inappropriate at graveside. Their mother gave them a warning glance before turning to follow the mourners back to a home that felt empty now, despite being full of people.

Over the years, Tina would wonder at how the interment seemed to mark the end of mourning, and everyone could enjoy a nice visit with the family and relatives, a cup of coffee and some sweets. Laughter, chatter, hugs and handshakes and it was all over...except for the family.

For over a year Maria wore black and was quiet and subdued. Sometimes, laughing and joking with the children she seemed to forget her grief, but then she quickly remembered it.

CHAPTER EIGHT

YOU MEAN WE'RE GETTING A NEW FATHER?

ONE YEAR AND SEVEN MONTHS AFTER THE DEATH OF HER husband, Maria Boldt had some stunning news for her oldest daughter. "Besides your Oma Driedeger, you are the first person I'm telling this to. I have met someone I care for, and we will be getting married," she said, matter-of-factly.

Looking back to that day, Tina couldn't remember whether she was surprised by the news, upset by it, or just accepted it as inevitable. Maria broke the news of the approaching nuptials to her other children with just as little fanfare. Second marriages were common in an era of limited health care and premature deaths.

"Children, you know how much I miss your father, but it's been very hard for me to take care of the farm by myself. I have decided I need someone to take your father's place."

Take his place? Someone would be filling the empty chair at the table? Tina asked the question none of the younger ones even thought of. "You mean we're getting a new father?"

"Well . . . yes," Her mother seemed unsure of how to proceed, but after a deep breath continued, "You remember Mr. David Schroeder who visits at your Oma Driedeger's home?"

Tina wasn't sure but nodded her head. She and the others waited for the next piece of shocking news.

"Mr. Schroeder has asked me to marry him, and I have said yes. The wedding will be next month in your Oma Driedeger's machine shed, and we will be inviting the aunts, uncles, and cousins. Oma has said he is a kind and gentle man and will take good care of us."

Children were not encouraged to question family decisions; the conversation was closed. Time would reveal everything.

Weddings were always exciting events, but Tina never thought her mother would be the next bride. She and her Aunt Helena discussed the news. The boys hardly seemed interested.

It was not until the children met their new father-to-be that they realized how strong blew the winds of change. David Schroeder's first visit to the Boldt house in Blumenau was understandably awkward; Maria played her role as genteel lady-of-the-house, confusing the boys who by turn acted speechlessly shy or boisterously rowdy.

In her best grown-up way, Tina shook hands with the rather ordinary-looking, curly-haired man their mother had chosen to marry. As the afternoon progressed, she began to feel she might like this person. His generous smile included everyone, even the over-excited boys. He brought with him a sense of confidence and amiable good-humour that soon put everyone at ease. Isaac and Cornelius were induced to say a few sensible words and stop acting like a pair of hellions. Tina relaxed and even enjoyed the afternoon.

Her biggest surprise was the person her new stepfather brought with him–his only daughter, Sara, a girl about her own age. Tina tried to think of something to say to this new sister, but the two stood uncomfortably silent until she and Aunt Helena hurried away to put fesper on the table.

Wedding preparations went ahead at lightning speed. The week before the wedding, Oma Driedeger's storage barn was emptied out, swept, and scrubbed as clean as it had ever been. Linens were washed, and cedar bows and flowers picked and stored. Tina helped Aunt Helena plan the meal, the boys helped set up tables and chairs, and Neta was given the job of arranging the greenery. It was a little like the funeral, but with less crying and nicer music.

Tina had forgotten how many aunts and uncles, half-brothers and sisters, and cousins once or twice removed were part of the family. Neta asked many times, "Who is that?" Tina gave up trying to remember the relationships and Neta stopped asking.

A second marriage was not as important as a first and the rules changed slightly. The bride never wore a white dress or veil. She might carry a small bouquet of garden flowers, and the groom wore his Sunday best suit with a ribbon lapel pin.

South Russian weather lived up to its reputation. The wedding day dawned clear and warm; it was going to be the perfect day. The flow of guests seemed never-ending. After the obligatory taking of vows and sermons of love and faithfulness, came the best part: visiting, meeting new family, children released from the bonds of propriety running wild through the orchards and fields.

Neighbours and ladies from the *Frauen Verein* removed their head gear and other articles of clothing that were causing discomfort, donned aprons and prepared to help serve the wedding *fesper*. They placed an abundance of food on the table: *pluma moos*, a fruit compote often served with cold ham and *zwieback*, the buttery rolls that were the hallmark of Mennonite cooking, and baked delicacies like *schnetki, rollkuchen* with watermelon in season, cookies and fruit *platz*. (No one remarked on the carefully washed and ironed tablecloths, now hidden under the feast.)

Before the meal, all guests joined in the singing of the melodic grace, *Nun danket Alle Gott mitt Herzen, Mund und Hände.* (Now Thank we all our God, with Hearts and Hands and Voices.)

They had much to be thankful for. In the year 1911, rain at the right time and warm summer days brought bountiful crops of grain, abundant fruits and vegetables from the gardens, and cattle grazing in belly-deep grass in the communal pastures. The blessings flowed.

The day ended with the happily exhausted guests taking their leave. Maria and David managed to steal away to their new family home for a few minutes of being alone together. They returned to say good-by to guests and help clear the remnants of the celebration in preparation for tomorrow's breakfast. The couple was expected to arrive bright and early the next morning to help prepare and serve the meal to departing guests, enduring the knowing looks from family and the whispered comments from David's buddies.

Only the very rich took wedding trips; most newlyweds were lucky to have a room to themselves. David made the move into the Boldt family home as his recently married oldest son and his wife needed a place to live and would occupy the Schroeder house in Landskrohn.

If the Boldt children had been apprehensive about having a new father, it was short-lived. It was a happy union. David Schroeder, their new father was younger than their own father had been. He brought a lightness and joyfulness into the house, more laughter, less furrow-browed warnings and strict enforcement of rules. Their mother smiled a lot and the children were allowed to entertain their friends without worry about noise or mess.

After getting past their initial awkwardness, Tina and Sara found lasting friendship. Tina loved her stepsister's flashing dark eyes and dimpled cheeks while Sara confessed that even as a child she had prayed for blonde hair and high cheek bones. Sara's sociable demeanour complimented Tina's quiet, thoughtful one. The girls' birthdays, being so close together, were celebrated in style. Their friendship was to last until time and distance parted them, many years later.

The question of what to call Mr. Schroeder was discussed in private by the Boldt children. "We can't call him Mr. Schroeder and only mother calls him David. He's not our father so we can't call him father . . ."

Neta solved the problem without even trying. She followed Sara's lead and called him Papa, and soon all the children, even Tina, were doing the same. All their lives he would be their Papa. They would remember the stories he told, the books he read to them, and the games he played with them. He would be their rock in every storm.

When their adventuresome stepfather came into their lives, they visited places they had only heard of before, starting with a trip to the warm beaches of the Sea of Azov, a world of dreams and rich people. It was the wedding trip David had planned for his new bride, taking with them five children under the age of thirteen. They would forever cherish the memory of that short but exciting trip. Some of their travels exposed them to the hustle and bustle of the city. David's father had owned a prosperous farm implement manufacturing business, and in his younger years David had visited Melitopal, Kharkov and even Kiev to purchase materials and parts for his father's factory. Cornelius and Isaac listened to his accounts of those visits and pleaded with him to take them there. The following summer David gave in to their pleading.

The family was beyond excited at the prospect of a visit to Kiev, although Maria vacillated between anticipation and anxiety. It was a long trip by rail and Maria, who had never been to any city bigger than Melitopal, had serious doubts about such an undertaking. David assured her he would take them only to the safest areas, where there were interesting things for the whole family to see. She relented, and when they found themselves on the smoke-belching passenger-train, she settled back into the leather-covered seat, determined to enjoy the adventure.

In Kiev, the inn they found was not far from the main train station, near the markets and parks. The boys stared open-mouthed at the shiny topless touring cars and the loud delivery trucks whizzing by on the streets, putting pedestrians in peril and startling plodding carriage horses. They took memorable rides on the huge, brown and gold tram that traveled up and down the main street, slowly enough for passengers to step on or off.

The highlight of the trip was a preview of the Zoological Gardens, which were almost ready to open. The children stared in wonder at animals they had only seen in books. Neta was disappointed there were no elephants but was thrilled when the leggy giraffe bent to nibble the bow in her hair. The boys offered bunches of dried grass to a zebra, while a lion in a far-off cage roared his anger at being locked up. Tina and Sara loved all the animals but hated that they would never again wander the grassy fields and forests of their native countries.

The last stop before the long train journey home was the general store owned by David's friend, Efim Golub. The store stretched through most of the lower floor of an ancient stone building in the busy market area. The children were amazed from the moment they stepped through the door. Where to look first? The store contained kitchenware and clothing, tools and toys, books and boots and all manner of exotic foods, but for the children the main attraction was the high-spirited owner who seemed to be everywhere at once, greeting customers, unpacking goods, manning the cash machine.

Isaac and Cornelius nudged each other and tried not to laugh when the full-bodied Efim greeted his friend David with strong-armed hugs and shouts of joy. "How many years is it since you used to come in here with your father? Twenty? Twenty-five more likely! Now my father is gone and yours too? Can you believe it, now we are the old ones?"

The family stood open-mouthed, listening to the two reminisce until the shopkeeper clapped the boys on the shoulder, nearly knocking Cornelius over and startling Isaac into dumbfounded silence.

"And where did you find these handsome young men? And these lovely ladies belong to you as well?"

When David introduced him to his daughter Sara and explained how he had acquired two sons, two more daughters and a lovely wife as well, Efim roared his approval and pronounced him a lucky man.

To celebrate the visit, the children were treated to the signature delicacy of the store's bakery, chocolate-dipped squares of halvah, the irresistible sesame confectionary usually reserved for special occasions. After enjoying the rare treat of ice cream served in small metal dishes with delicate silver spoons, they would have been satisfied to spend the rest of the day sampling the endless array of sweets. Reluctantly, the family left the store and its boisterous owner to board the train for home.

David took pleasure in teasing the boys when they got home. "All that time and money spent on a trip to Kiev and all you can tell your friends about is the sweet treats given to you by my friend, the Jewish shop-keeper. I could just as easily have taken you to Oma Driedeger's kitchen and have her make *rollkuchen* or *pfeffernuesse* for you!"

The boys were never quite sure if their stepfather was serious or not. Maria grinned at her husband's teasing and assured him the family would never forget the museums and parks and especially the Zoological gardens.

Little did they know the trip marked a milestone, a turning point in their lives.

Most of their trips, to either Maria or David's many relatives, were of much shorter duration and not nearly as exciting. Not all Mennonites lived in the villages, home to the hard-working farming middle classes. Papa Schroeder had relatives among the wealthy owners of great tracts of land, estates as they were known, often with romantic descriptive German names like *Grosstannen* or *Silberweide*.

1915-1917

Papa Schroeder occasionally took his new family to visit the grand summer home of their well-to-do Penner relatives on the *Sommerfluss* estate, cared for during the winter by managers and hired workers.

Tina and Sara admired the elegant clothing worn by their sophisticated Penner cousins but felt the family to be snobbish and condescending to their country kin. The many rooms of their home were filled with heavy, ornate furniture, gilt-edged pictures of bucolic country scenes and endless bric-a-brac which, Truda Penner, the lady of the house, pointed out with considerable pride.

They were even invited to take a ride in the shiny black Opel car, stored in a special part of the machine shed. Both Tina and Sara declined.

"I said no because I thought I might dirty that velvet-covered seat, or that my shoes would muddy the floor," Tina whispered to her sister later.

"I really wanted to go, but I didn't know whether I should sit or stand, or how to act in that fancy vehicle. I thought cousin Greta would make fun of me for doing something wrong. She's only two years older than I, but she acts like I know nothing, and she knows everything." Sara's eyes held an amused gleam. "If they ask us again, I'll just watch her and do what she does."

"Did you hear what she said to me when she saw the collar that Mama crocheted for my blue dress?" demanded Neta.

Sara shrugged her shoulders and said, "No, and you should not listen to what that conceited girl says, either."

"She said they have their clothes made by a seamstress in Kiev. She is in demand by all the best-dressed people in the city."

"Nothing is nicer than the beautiful things Mama makes. Who cares what Greta says?" Tina gently rearranged Neta's collar and patted her sister's cheek. "So, forget all about it."

Tina remembered the chat, not because of Neta's concerns, but because of a conversation she had overheard coming from the Penner's sitting room when only the men were present. The topic on everyone's lips was the war. Russia was at war with Germany. Tina had learned more about the war in the last year. She knew that although young Mennonite men were exempt from military service, they were expected to serve either in the medical corps or forestry service. Since the beginning of the war, many young men had boarded the troop trains to become part of the non-combatant Medical Corps. They would be riding the hospital trains to care for wounded soldiers being transported between the front and Moscow, to military hospitals along the way. Most felt this was the best way to show loyalty to their Motherland without engaging in battle.

With conversations dominated by rumours on the state of the war, the visit to the estate marked another milestone. Tina remembered her sense of foreboding as she listened to the hushed conversation coming from the Penner's sitting room.

She never forgot her Papa Schroeder's words, "I have no doubt this will lead to civil war. It will not be over until more Russian blood is shed. Pray to God He will protect us from what is to come."

It was the last time they were to visit the grand home of their relatives at the estate at *Sommerfluss*, neither would they ever ride in the luxurious black Opel, as the following year it was requisitioned by the government for use in the war effort.

Rumours and warnings of government requisition of property and goods grew louder, while smoke-belching trains loaded with troops crossed the land, heading for the front. The soldiers were excited in their ignorance; armed for battle, they were invincible and assured of victory. They had no doubt peace would soon return.

The villagers took more notice when the rumours began to change from whispers to shouts reporting disorder and chaos. Warnings of unrest seeped into every conversation as the demands of the Russian people became known. They wanted bread, they wanted justice, they wanted freedom from tyranny and the ability to provide their families with the necessities of life. When the Tsar abdicated in the early months of 1917 and the government was over-thrown, Tina remembered her Papa's talk of civil war.

The question was asked, but no one had the answer, "Who is in charge now that the Tsar is gone?"

Hope grew when a provisional government was installed. Could it be that a new government would really listen to the people, hear their concerns, and give them the opportunities to build new lives?

Turmoil was building in the villages. There were rumours of roving bands of thieves thundering into the quiet of the villages, hooves clattering, harnesses jangling, dark unkempt men waving weapons and shouting, leaping from foam-lathered horses and pushing aside the terror-filled residents. Were the rumours true? The possibility of armed invaders overrunning their peaceful villages, sent fear into every heart. So many questions. *Who were these people and what did they want?*

The countryside was flooded with the homeless, the hungry, the lawless and the desperate. Russia was running out of clothing, ammunition, even food for her soldiers, who, injured, abandoned, and hungry, began deserting in droves. Desperate individuals were roaming the country looking for food and lodgings, while anarchist gangs took what they felt was their right to take.

Tina's brothers, Cornelius and Isaac, were too young for the mandatory medical or forestry non-combative service. Next door to the Schroeder's, however, in a large brick house lived two of the four Lentz brothers with their widowed mother. The two youngest, Franz and Heinrich were the right age for conscription. These deployments, reserved for the sons of pacifist Mennonites, were considered lucky. Still, their families watched with dread as their young men left to go to war, not with guns or bayonets, but with bandages and medicine. For medics and ambulance attendants, gathering up the dead and wounded and listening to the unearthly screams of the horribly injured was nothing to be envied.

Tina watched as her neighbour Franz Lentz and seven others she didn't know well, boarded the horse-drawn wagon on their way to the train station in Lichtenau, and from there to an unknown destination. The boys smiled and waved. "We'll be back soon!" they called. There were sad faces and tears among the families who watched them go.

That night, Tina had a dream that was to recur many times throughout her life. She stood on the top of a hill that stretched far and away from her, heading down, down into a milling darkness of clouds. Something compelled her to start down the hill, the grade getting steeper with every step. Soon she was running, faster, faster, the countryside a blur, faster and faster until her feet could not keep up the momentum and she hurtled onto the rocky soil, her heart pounding, sweat pouring from her face. She woke in a panic, clammy with the pounding rhythm of her heart. She was never able to see if there was light somewhere beyond the clouds.

CHAPTER NINE

A BASKET OF ZWIEBACK

December 1917

LIKE SMOKE FROM A WILDFIRE, RUMOURS CONTINUED TO SPREAD from one village to the next, frightening tales of homes being invaded by bandits and thugs, laughing and joking as they rummaged through drawers and cupboards, taking what they wanted and trampling the rest.

Schönsee, Furstenau, the distance between the affected villages and Blumenau was diminishing every day. Rumour became reality in Blumenau just a month before Christmas.

Sounds of thundering hoof-beats and shouting were the first warning. Residents rushed to see what the commotion was, only to dash back into their homes, terrified, gathering children, locking doors, praying for protection.

In the Schroeder house, the girls and their parents drew the blinds and made sure every door was locked. While David tried to see what was happening, the others huddled together, feeling a sense of helplessness. Maria was thankful Isaac and Cornelius were away from home and would be gone for several hours.

The family crowded into the back room of the house, in disbelief, as the sounds of the chaos robbed their home of peace and quiet. Maria and the girls held on to each other, their closeness a shield from any intrusion.

Neta, held protectively in the strong arms of her Papa, looked frail and small. "We will be all right," he murmured, his lips pressed against the silken hair of his youngest stepchild. "God will protect us. We will keep our faith strong that our Heavenly Father will shield us from harm."

Neta sobbed in fear, clinging to her parents even as the echo of the turmoil drew nearer. The ground shook with the force of a horde, while the sounds of laughter, screams, commanding voices and sporadic gun fire reverberated through the house. The tenuous sense of relief they felt when the turmoil swept by was replaced by horror when another followed close behind.

A pack of marauders slowed to a stop at Bee-Keeper Janzen's beautifully landscaped yard from where the shouts, and the screaming seemed to go on forever. After what felt like hours, the echoes of the melee grew fainter and receded into the distance, beyond their homes and out of the village.

Tina and Sara lifted a corner of the blind to see how the houses next door had fared. A mess of scattered goods littered the street—clothing, pots, furniture, broken dishes, an over-turned wheelbarrow, and tools from the shed. Shocked residents came out of their homes, trepidation in every step. The sturdy figure of

Mrs. Janzen stumbled from the house, hugging a white bundle to her chest. Her face was blank with shock as she picked her way around the scattered remnants of the raid, before blindly heading away.

Maria recognized shock when she saw it and hurried after the trembling woman. "Are you all right? Did they hurt you? What about the rest of the family?"

Mrs. Janzen seemed too shaken to respond, burying her face in the lace-trimmed bundle of cloth she held. Finally, between sobs she was able to tell the tale. "I was the only one home. They took everything from my Frieda's linen chest, all the blankets and sheets and pillows. I tried to stop them. They just laughed and took what they wanted. They grabbed all the bread I had just baked; it wasn't even cold yet. They just took bites of it and threw it into a sack. They broke my good dishes. They took Heinrich's winter coat and gloves. What will he wear when it gets cold?"

Maria tried to comfort the hysterical woman who was still holding the tattered piece of tablecloth she had lovingly created for her oldest daughter's wedding chest. People milled around, feeling lost, bereft, and afraid. When they were sure the invaders had left, the community gathered in the church to discuss what had happened. The first task was to ensure that no one was missing, injured, or needing help.

Reverend Heidebrecht and the schoolteacher, Herman Wiebe, took charge and the group settled down. From the pulpit came the prayer: "Heavenly Father, we thank You for keeping Your sheltering hand over us. What we lost is trifling, what we kept is our lives and the lives of our loved ones. Please give us strength and courage to face what is to come."

Spontaneously the group broke out in the hymn so often sung in church on Sundays, U*nter deinem sanften Fittig find ich Frieden, Trost und Ruh.* (Under your protecting wings, I find comfort, peace and rest.)

A sense of bewilderment and dread invaded the village. No one knew what to do next, or how to protect themselves. Many residents had already taken some precautions, hiding grain, food and precious belongings. Others could not believe the rumours and tried to carry on as usual, until reality taught them otherwise.

Every day brought reports of invasions of homes and injury to occupants. Horrified citizens heard stories of women and girls being hurt and abused. Parents tried to think of ways to protect their families.

David Schroeder's pale face and unshaven cheeks gave him an unfamiliar look of despair as he gathered Tina, Sara and Neta around him. "Girls, I need to talk with you. Never in my life would I have thought this conversation with you would be necessary."

Tina felt a shortness of breath. What could be coming next?

"If you ever see men you don't know trying to come into the house, you all have to immediately find a safe place to go. In this house the storage room behind the pantry is probably the safest place because most people don't know it's there."

"But Papa," protested Neta, "It's so dark in there. I'm afraid to go in there by myself."

"Yes, but you have to be brave. We will make sure there's a place for you to curl up, with a blanket and some of your dollies to keep you company. You probably won't be alone, but you will need to be quiet and wait until someone comes for you." David hoped that what he was telling his daughters was right, and that he was not putting them into more danger.

The entire world was on the move. Destitute soldiers were returning to turmoil from a lost war, taking what they felt their military service entitled them to. Citizens of the Russian villages, always living on the edge of famine, were the hardest hit. Food and supplies were harder and harder to come by. Families, children, and old people found themselves in evermore precarious situations, fleeing from the hordes who threatened and tormented anyone who crossed their path.

Not even the small insignificant Mennonite village of Blumenau was immune to incursions of hungry citizens. Strangers were more often seen, their ragged clothes and wan complexions telling the story. Russian villagers had often come to the Mennonite villages looking for work, looking for a handout or something to steal, but this was more ominous. Every evening, Papa locked the barn doors and the door between the kitchen and the long barn passage-way.

"There are little children out there," pleaded Maria, "We have to do something. They need a place to sleep. Something to eat."

Papa's usually sunny face darkened. "Maria, how would we have room for all these people? Can you feed them all?" Never had Tina heard such stern words from her loving stepfather.

"No, of course not, but we can help some of them."

"How will you keep them all from coming in when we have no more room? What will you give them when we've given them all our food?" Papa's voice was sharp and insistent.

Maria, though she knew he was right, could not stop fretting about the condition of hungry children. David's one concession was to set a basket of roasted *zwieback*, behind the fence. Someone was sure to find them.

The village slept uneasily that night and those that followed. By New Year's Day it had lived through four more incursions of gangs of thieves, crude unkempt men, laughing and joking, making obscene gestures to shy young girls who cringed from their touch. Reports of young women attacked by gangs of thugs, raped and horribly injured, even murdered, swept through the villages.

Villagers found ingenious places to hide things, mostly food-stuff: floor, salt, yeast, eggs, potatoes, turnips, carrots, onions, and anything edible. Clothing was stuffed into sacks and hidden in dark cellar corners where the evil trespassers were reluctant to go. Hidden among the stuffed sacks were precious items, photos, a rare silver watch or a fine gold chain given as a wedding gift. When this became known to them, the dark cellar corners were the first to be searched.

The Schroeder house was invaded twice during that time, losing bags of oatmeal, flour and canned goods from the cellar. So far, no one had been injured. They feared they would not always be so fortunate. Their premonitions were justified one morning when about a dozen, dark, bedraggled men pushed their way into the house, shouting and laughing. Shocked and unprepared, David and Isaac found themselves backed into a corner facing several armed intruders. It was well known that taunting grins and laughter could quickly become serious when the bandits were challenged, but David's only thought was for his family. "Take what you want, it's yours, just leave my family alone, my wife and my children. They've done nothing to hurt anyone."

David's voice was drowned out by the noise of the upheaval leaving him feeling helpless and ashamed while the belligerents spread through the house taking what they wanted.

When Sara realized what was happening, she remembered her Papa's instructions about going to the safe room but also remembered nine-year old Neta had been playing with her dolls in the *kleinestubbe*. Should she try to sneak into the small back room, hoping no one would see her, or do nothing and take the chance her sister would not be found? Sara knew she could not leave Neta's welfare to chance.

She edged her way to the door, hoping to make her way down the hallway without being noticed. The room was only steps away when with knee-weakening shock she saw the shadowy outline of two men who had stepped from behind the door to the barn, blocking her passage. The smell of stale tobacco smoke and garlic almost made her gag, an odor that would forever take her back to the moment their presence filled the hallway.

The two shabby young men were joyful at meeting a beautiful young girl in the empty hallway. Sara held her breath as they laughingly reached for her. The calloused, grimy hands of one of them touched the fabric of her dress, letting the material flow through his fingers. She shivered as the other one, eyes shining, and lips slobbering, stroked her hair and caressed her shoulder. She squeezed her eyes to shut out the sight of the bristly black hairs on his neck, and then realized this was not the time to show weakness.

"Stop! Don't touch me!"

Her dark eyes flashed as she warned them to keep their distance. They crowded in closer, but Sara stood her ground and grabbed the first thing that came to hand when they refused to back off. It happened to be a brass paperweight from the desk beside the door. For a young woman, Sara packed an unexpected punch and landed a hefty wallop on the nose of the one who was unlucky enough to be within her reach. No one was more surprised than Sara to see blood pouring from his nose, down his chin, soaking his already grimy shirt. He tried in vain to staunch the flow, then stumbled from the room. He was followed by his partner, who shot Sara a warning look as he eyed the brass object in her hand. Sara heard shouts of laughter from the other room; a bloody nose at the hand of a girl was obviously the source of great hilarity. Sara's heart was racing, but she felt a sense of victory as she and Neta made their quick way to the pantry hideaway. Neta was frozen with fear, but safe.

The marauders began leaving, carrying pillow cases filled with goods and household articles, laughing and joking as they admired what they had taken. The taunting voices of the three men holding David and his stepson prisoner in the *eckstubbe* could still be heard. Maria and the girls crowded into the pantry hideaway where the noises of the mayhem were less obvious, but the dull thuds of objects being thrown, and furniture being overturned could still be heard. Neta huddled close to her mother and covered her ears.

Maria's knuckles showed white and her voice was barely a whisper, dreading what might follow. "Please, please, Lord Jesus, keep my family safe."

Tina's voice was shaky with relief, when the sounds of the uproar faded. "I think they've gone."

It was not until David and Isaac were heard outside the pantry door that they all breathed more easily. For a few moments more they held tightly to each other, shaky with relief that everyone was safe.

Maria noticed the pallor on David's face and was shocked at what she saw in his expression. Shame was written on his downcast face. "I couldn't stop them. They just laughed and flashed their weapons and threw things around the room, like it was all one big joke."

Tina felt rage sweep through her body and was sure Sara felt the same as she tried to comfort her father after his degrading experience. "They should be ashamed, threatening helpless people! How can you stop them when they have guns and you don't?"

When his breathing slowed, and his heart returned to its normal steady beat, David held Sara close. "You were the bravest one today. Thank God you are safe."

Cornelius felt guilt-ridden that he had not been home to help his family but was amazed to hear his step-sister had won out over such odds. "You taught those two hooligans a good lesson. People will be calling you 'Strong-arm Sara' after this." Cornelius's attempt at lightening the mood drew a very small smile from Sara. There was little enough to find humour in.

It was a downtrodden group that followed the garden path to church that Sunday. When Elder Toews asked for protection in the New Year, "Heavenly Father, we thank-you for bringing us safely through this tumultuous year of revolution and war, and we pray that 1918 will bring peace to our troubled land," the congregation uttered a hearty "Amen."

CHAPTER TEN

THE BREAD IN YOUR CUPBOARD

1918

THE NEW YEAR SENT FRESH RUMOURS FLYING FROM VILLAGE to village. The lands of the rich were going to be expropriated by the Bolshevik government. It was called "collectivization", but by any name, it meant what they had owned and toiled for would be taken from them.

The warnings flew on eagle's wings, hovering over the homes of rich and poor alike, beating out the ominous messages, "Keep your children close. Dress in your poorest clothes. Hide your valuables, keep your horses and cattle out of sight, and store your foodstuff in the root cellar."

Papa Schroeder's rich Penner relatives were among the first estate owners to feel the heavy hand of the Bolshevik government.

"Truda Penner and her daughter Greta were given an hour to gather their belongings and leave *Sommerfluss*. They couldn't think of what to take so they left a lot of important things behind." Papa Schroeder shook his head in resigned disbelief even as he shared the news with his family.

Tina and Sara couldn't help but wonder if the wardrobe of fine clothing purchased in Kiev would have been taken or left behind.

"I feel sorry for them even though they look down on the poorer people like us." said Tina.

Sara wasn't as generous, "They'll find out how it feels to be poor."

Maria Schroeder shook her head at her daughters, "Girls, don't speak too soon, we could be the next ones to lose everything."

"We aren't rich, what have we got that the government would want?" wondered Tina.

"Your horses and cows, your chickens and pigs, the wheat in your bin and the bread in your cupboard." Isaac said. Being the oldest of Tina's brothers, he considered himself quite worldly wise, having listened to the tales told by travelers and residents alike.

The same questions were on everybody's mind. Will it happen to us? Will our land be taken? Where will we go?

No one considered themselves rich. Most of the village farms were small holdings barely large enough to provide the family with a living. Families worked together for the good of all and shared a house until one of the older sons or daughters was able to buy their own land or find work in the city.

Cornelius brought more shocking news. "In Heirschau, a gang of bandits stole from almost every house and murdered six people who tried to stop them. They think it might have been that

Russian bandit Nestor Makhno and his gang. They are on the move in the northern colonies. They robbed people of whatever they could carry and killed those that got in their way!"

"Dear Jesus, what will happen next?" Maria Schroeder's wail of fear sent chills through everyone's body. "That man is a devil! I've heard he will stop at nothing!"

Isaac had heard the tales. Nestor Makhno, short in stature but large in reputation, preached anarchism and the law of to the victor go the spoils. "He hates the Mennonites. If he comes here, we are doomed. He says there is no law in the country that can keep him from taking what he wants. He will fight anyone who stands in his way."

For a moment the family was paralyzed with fear, then Maria and David went into action. "Neta has to be protected from all this talk of robbing and killing. Tina, take her over to Tante Lentz, maybe she will keep her occupied for a while."

Tante Lentz, their neighbour, mother of four boys, and grandmother of three, highly respected matriarch of Blumenau, well-educated and wealthy in her own right, was always available to advise and assist. Her husband had passed away nearly ten years ago, when her youngest son, Franz, was sixteen, leaving the villagers to wonder which of the widowers, who suddenly seemed to have pressing business in the vicinity, would have the temerity to pay suit to the formidable lady. Not beautiful but handsome and intelligent, she could have taken her pick of men seeking a competent, financially secure woman with whom to share their lives. She chose none of them, opting instead to run her property with the help of her two youngest sons, Heinrich and Franz.

Maria was one of the few people who could say she knew her neighbour well and considered her a friend. Neta often accompanied her mother on visits to the imposing lady who, having no daughters of her own, had taken a liking to the bright, friendly little girl. Tina had accompanied her mother a few times, but Tante Lentz's two handsome, outgoing sons, being older than she, made her feel shy and tongue-tied.

Tina and Neta hurried down the path through a hedge of lilac bushes to the Lentz house. Tina was taken aback when her knock on the door was answered not by Tante Lentz but by Franz, who had just returned from the six-month tour of duty with the Medical Corps.

Tina saw at first glance that this was not the genial neighbour she had known from childhood. His blonde good looks were as striking as ever, but a shadow of gravity or was it sadness, had been drawn across his face. In a moment, as recognition passed between them, the shadow was replaced by his normal, neighbourly smile of welcome.

"Hello, Neta and Tina! Come in, come in. This is no time to be standing out in the open for long. One never knows what's hiding in the bushes."

Tina was surprised she felt no shyness. "Welcome home. It's so good to see you back. I didn't realize you were home. Mama was hoping Neta could stay with your mother for a while until we have finished organizing the food supplies into the cellar."

"Well, it may not do much good hiding things, those thugs always seem to find something they want, but you're right, we don't have to make it easy for them. Come, Neta, Emma is looking after Heinrich's bunch and could use some help." Franz waited while Neta went to find the housemaid and her charges, then spoke the warning every young woman had heard so often. "Be very careful when you're outside. Don't let those beasts catch you alone."

"Believe me, Papa has warned us girls many times. It's really sad that we can't even visit our neighbours without worrying about our safety."

"Come on, I'm going to walk you home."

"It's just a short distance, I'll be all right."

But Franz was already at the door. "Come on, I'll feel better if you aren't alone."

He didn't linger at her door, but after assuring her he would bring Neta back later, turned to hurry back to do whatever he could to keep his own home safe. Tina couldn't help but wonder what that would be. As a pacifist, his faith did not allow him to take up the sword, as it were, yet she knew many Mennonite men had every intention of doing what was necessary to keep their families safe.

How often had she heard someone say, "If they take my possessions, I can live with that, but if they attack my family, I will use a gun or an ax, anything I have, to keep them safe."

Tina watched Franz as his long, firm strides took him back to his mother, his brother and his nephews, and she knew without asking that Franz would do what was necessary to keep his family safe.

Back in the shelter of her home, Tina helped her parents find safe places for food, clothing and other items important to their family's wellbeing. They did everything they could think of to find a safe place. Bags of grain were divided into smaller containers, flour was re-bagged in burlap sacks or tins, hiding places were disguised as rain barrels. The dark kitchen cellar was still the safest place, as many of the marauders were reluctant to enter the dark under-ground caverns that might hide more than just clothes or food.

How could their world have changed from the peacefulness of the fifteenth birthday party to terror and peril just four years later? Every day, every week, every month, brought new threats, rumours of invasions, arrests, and murders of anyone deemed wealthy or resistant in any way to the new Bolshevik regime.

Bandits were an almost daily occurrence somewhere in the villages. Who presented the most danger, the brutal hangers-on of the Russian anarchist Nestor Makhno, the cruel and cold-blooded recruits of the newly minted Red Army or the fanatical White Army militants desperately hanging on to the status quo? As they ranged back and forth across the country, one could only guess who would be the enemy of the day.

What happened in Katherina Lentz's home one early February morning was so frightening that the whole village was revolted and terror stricken. Not only bandits, homeless peasants, and various mobs of unknown origin were using the villages as a

source of food and supplies, but also riotous companies of Red
or White Army soldiers. No one would forget the day a troop
entered the village, bandoliers jangling, weapons in hand.

Katherina was in the kitchen preparing the midday meal for her
three grandchildren, who in the periods of turmoil and trouble
were spending most of their time in their ancestral home. She
was caught off guard by the band of soldiers who thundered
down the peaceful tree-lined street and into her snow-covered
yard. She heard the sound of tethered horses in the barn, the
tromping of feet and loud shouts as they stormed through the
passageway and into her kitchen, fragrant with the smell of the
chicken soup on the stove.

She had thought of what might happen if someone broke in
when she was alone in the house with her grandchildren. She
had long ago decided that a bunch of poverty-stricken peasants
didn't scare her, and if it was Nestor Makhno, she would lay the
law down to that ignorant, lawless little Russian pip-squeak.
The reality took her by surprise when it was neither peasants
nor anarchists who invaded her home, but Red Army soldiers
looking for a meal.

There were about a dozen of them, young, cocky individuals,
probably in a position of authority for the first time in their
lives, armed with a variety of weapons, ammunition jingling on
their chests. Their presence crowded the large kitchen and filled
it with the rank smell of horse and gun powder.

"We timed it just right! Grandmother, what are you cooking?" they demanded. "We haven't eaten for hours. Come, set the table. You have hungry visitors! Cook, woman, cook."

Katherina felt a surge of fury building up inside her as another hungry horde treated her home as their own. "I've made only enough food for these children. They're my grandchildren and I have barely enough to feed them. Everyone has taken what we have."

The steely-eyed captain of the troop raised his hand to quiet the unruly mob. He left no doubt as to who was in charge; his smart uniform, emblazoned with the red star, and the shiny black boots he wore set him apart from the rag-tag group of obviously new recruits. Silence fell, as with an ominous tone he answered the old lady who stood determinedly erect, even as she began to regret her words.

"I understand, Grandmother, you have a lot of mouths to feed." His words were conciliatory, but his actions sent a shockwave of fear through her whole body. In a lightening move, his gun was in his hand. The barrel of the monstrous weapon was being pressed to the forehead of Peter, the blonde, blue-eyed cherub of a child who, just seconds before, had been waving his spoon in happy anticipation of his favorite food. "Why don't I just get rid of this one, then you won't have so many?"

Katherina Lentz felt a choking fear, heart-stopping and knee-weakening. "Please, please, I will find something for you to eat, please, please don't hurt him." In a quavering voice, she pleaded and begged as she never had before.

Katherina would forever remember the malicious smirk on the captain's face as his finger tightened on the trigger. The moment stretched into eternity as the barrel of the gun pressed more roughly onto the tiny boy's pale forehead.

With hardly a glance in her direction, the captain slowly lowered his weapon and holstered it. "That's better, grandmother, now get busy!"

With shaking hands, she began to prepare pancakes, a food she knew could be made quickly and feed many. Young Nicky tried in vain to comfort his little brother whose high-pitched shrieks now filled the room.

The captain made a feint towards his weapon. "Shut him up!" he ordered. The malevolence in his voice made Katherina's blood run cold.

It took supreme effort to keep the quiver out of her voice. "Nicky, take Peter to Emma and get her to lay him down for his afternoon nap. You may as well take Heinie with you as well."

"Yes, Oma." There was relief in every word as he hurried to take his little brothers out of the room.

The crepe pancakes, liberally doused with watermelon syrup, seemed to please the now jovial group. The tin barrel of flour was nearly empty, when finally, they had had enough.

At a signal from their captain and with barely a glance, they left. Only one of the well-fed individuals had any words for her on his way out, "That was quite good, but I just can't eat this one." And he tossed his last remaining pancake to the dog.

Alone in her kitchen, the strong, the fearless, the indomitable Katherina folded her still shaking hands and thanked God for the life of little Peter.

CHAPTER ELEVEN

FAITH OF OUR FATHERS

April 1918

THE VILLAGERS WERE STILL SHUDDERING AT THE MEMORY OF the nightmare invasion of Tante Lentz's home when rumours were again flying. Russia was losing the war, more and more soldiers were deserting, ammunition was in short supply, clothing, even socks and boots were impossible to get. Soldiers were suffering from lack of food and medical treatment. Hundreds of them had abandoned their posts and had begun the long walk home. Hungry, homeless and injured soldiers huddled in doorways of abandoned buildings in the cities and villages. The citizenry eyed the wild-eyed, often belligerent men and ran from them, trusting no one.

To the tangled labyrinth of warring factions was added one more menace as conflicting rumours spread through the colonies. "The Germans are coming, and the Reds are taking vengeance on the village Mennonites."

"Don't believe it. The Reds have withdrawn and Halbstadt is empty. Our liberators are here. We are saved!" What to believe?

Out of the mist on a rainy morning in April, in the cities of Halbstadt and Melitopal, on troop trains belching smoke and steam, a new army arrived. Not unruly gangs, stampeding, shouting and threatening, but uniformed, smart in orderly phalanxes. Word spread through the villages, help is here! We are saved! The German army has arrived to rout them all–the Reds, the Whites, the bandits, the Makhno's!

Colonel Fredrich Mensch explained their presence to the council leaders of the cities and villages. In brisk German, the language spoken by the transplanted Mennonites, he made it quite clear, "The Bolshevik government, via the Treaty of Brest Litovsk, has ceded this territory to Germany as a way of ending Russian participation in this confounded war."

A hundred questions were asked, Colonel Mensch could answer only a few, "This means you are under German rule, which seems right because of our common language. We will protect you from the parade of thieves and bandits that have been terrorizing your communities. For you this is a positive development."

The questions asked by the council members were in everyone's mind. "Will you fight for us? Will you be here to drive the Red Army back?"

"We will help you do what is necessary." Ambiguous answers left people skeptical and unsure, but for the moment, with breathing space. This was an army the German-speaking Mennonites could understand and communicate with.

This army was neat and militarily disciplined, and under the leadership of Fredrich Mensch, a dozen of them would be billeted in Blumenau. Some of the villagers felt a kinship with the young German soldiers even though the newcomers were the enemy of their adopted homeland. The German army seemed to view the villagers not as enemies, but as misguided compatriots. For most residents, whatever the reason for their presence, it was a reprieve from thieves and gangs. For others, despite the orderly appearance of these blond, blue-eyed young men, their presence was just one more complication, possibly putting the Mennonites squarely in the category of traitor.

Four young soldiers were billeted in the Schroeder house. Though they were clean and sharply dressed, their presence soiled the walls and windows, caused the curtains to hang crookedly and the floor mats to wrinkle under their feet. They were in the glove left behind on the table, the hat hanging on the hook, the metallic button on the floor. Maria eyed them suspiciously and warned her girls to stay well away from them. Sometimes Tina wished they would just leave, even though their presence meant safety from intruders.

Sara wedged a chair against the bedroom door and brought a chamber pot for Neta, so she wouldn't have to leave the room at night. Tina slept on a mattress on the floor with the dog beside her giving them all a fleeting sense of safety, knowing his shrill barks could awaken the whole house. Cornelius and Isaac slept in the barn, having vacated their small room for the soldiers.

Tina listened to the conversation around the kitchen table when the soldiers were away, when family and neighbours could speak freely. David Schroeder, being the senior member of the family, was respected and listened to even by other neighbours and friends. Franz Lentz became part of the discussion, as his experience with the Medical Corps gave his opinions the validation of firsthand knowledge. The youth of the brothers, Cornelius and Isaac, gave them the privilege of making comments and asking questions others were reluctant to ask, afraid of showing their naivete or ignorance.

It was David who asked the question no one was willing to address. "What will happen if Germany loses the war? We are welcoming them as saviours. Sooner or later they will pack up and go back to Germany, leaving us to be seen as traitors."

Isaac respected his stepfather's views, but this time he had his own opinion. "Russia has given up; her soldiers are coming home, ragged and starving. Why wouldn't Germany win?"

David read every newspaper, outdated or not, which found its way into this isolated corner of civilization. "Germany is fighting on many fronts. Her enemies are united in their effort to end this war. I believe Germany's days are numbered. I can only wonder how much more blood will be shed before this is finally over."

Franz's normally genial expression became dark and fierce. Was he remembering the face of his nephew, little Peter whose blood had so nearly stained the floor of the safest place in his world, his grandmother's kitchen? "Whatever happens, whether Germany wins or loses, I will do what I have to do to keep my family safe."

David filled in an uncomfortable silence with a suddenly accusatory tone. "You are talking *Selbstshutz*, aren't you, Franz? These Germans are convincing you to take up arms."

Selbstschutz–self-defense. The question of whether to carry weapons to meet aggression with aggression, or to trust in God's promise of protection, caused much disagreement in the Mennonite community.

Like many of them, Franz felt caught in the middle. "I believe in the faith of my Fathers. I won't join an army, but I can't just sit by and let bandits and thieves come into my home and threaten my family."

"Franz, be careful of what the German military is encouraging you to do. You know sooner or later they will leave. Will the *Selbstschutz* forces be strong enough to stand between your family and the Bolsheviks who will treat you as a traitor? You will be trading one enemy for another."

The question dominated every conversation and divided the congregations as nothing had ever done. The young men who saw the results of theft and murder were often of one mind. "God will help us if we help ourselves."

Franz's dilemma tugged at Tina's heart when she remembered how close young Peter had come to losing his life. Had God held His sheltering hand over the little boy, or did the well-decorated military man have some shred of compassion that had prevented him from killing an innocent child?

Soon, little boys in the village were playing soldier with stick guns and tin hats. The German soldiers laughed and teased them and showed them the right way to carry a gun. The elders shook their heads and warned the boys to stop their silly games. It was no longer a game when young men began to look to the German soldiers for weapons, and for training in their use.

The German soldiers seemed to treat their time in the villages much like a holiday, chatting up shy Mennonite girls and explaining the finer points of soldiering to eager young men. In many villages, the Germans planned festivals with music and dancing, which was something the puritan Mennonites had never done. Tina and Sara kept their distance from the festivities, feeling shy and uncomfortable among the gregarious men whose joking and loud laughter was unfamiliar to them. Russian girls working in Mennonite homes, however, heartily joined in, causing their Mennonite bosses to warn them of the dangers of cavorting with strange young men.

Tina could not help but be curious about the foreign, yet somehow familiar-looking, young German soldiers. Their fine German accent made her colloquial low-German sound flat and crude. She spoke respectfully to them, but listened to Maria who reminded her, "They are not your friends. Their allegiance is not to Russia. They are the enemy. Even if they keep us safe for now, I will be glad when they are gone."

For Sara, the smell of tobacco smoke and the sight of a hand-rolled cigarette held between yellow-stained fingers still brought back the confrontation in the barn hallway. Spending time in the kitchen, baking the buttery-rich *zwieback*, preparing the thick tomato and cabbage *borscht* or the deep-fried ground beef *kotleten* with boiled potatoes, gave her the excuse she needed to avoid sitting down at the table with the overly friendly young soldiers.

For Isaac and Cornelius, new duties were instituted. Though both were still too young to join the Selbstshutz, they took their turn standing guard at strategic places in the villages, and with other young men they practiced handling weapons. Like most of the people, they rationalized the practice. The weapons were only for protection and would not be used for assault. The line between defense and offence was narrowing.

David was relieved to turn his thoughts to other, more mundane things. "It's almost time to seed the wheat and barley and we don't have enough seed. The seeder needs some repairs. I haven't been able to find parts, so I will have to see what I can do about that. And I still need to go back to Halbstadt to try to find some more seed wheat."

"Papa, Isaac and I can do that. You have enough to do here."

Isaac, being the oldest son, felt strongly about doing his share. "Yes, we can. It will have to be today as I've volunteered to stand guard tomorrow night."

"You have almost no training with weapons. What will you do?" Maria's voice was strained and her relief at the change of subject had been short lived.

"I won't carry a weapon; I will be with someone who will. I will be the helper and carry messages between guards."

Maria kept her thoughts to herself, but Isaac's assurances made her feel only slightly better. The thought of her son standing guard in the middle of the night, with or without a weapon, had already caused her many a sleepless night.

For David, a less controversial topic of conversation was always welcome. "Tina and Sara, the boys may not be back in time for milking, so I guess you will have to fill in. Maria, the Russian girls I hired to help with the gardening should be here today."

"What can I do?" asked Neta not to be left out.

"I saved the most important job for you, Neta. Collecting the eggs and making *ruhrei* for midday lunch. Don't forget, I like my lunch tea with sugar."

Neta laughed. Everyone knew Papa liked sugar with his tea.

David and Maria watched with trepidation as the boys hitched the horse to the light wagon in preparation for the trip to Halbstadt to find seed grain. German vehicles on the road discouraged gangs and made the roads safer for ordinary citizens, but Maria still felt anxious about allowing her sixteen and seventeen-year-old sons to make the twelve-kilometer trip alone. She would be relieved when they were safely back home. The boys had been reminded to keep a close watch for anyone who showed too much interest in either the horse or the wagon. David assured her the boys knew all the safety measures to take and would, no doubt, be home sooner than expected. His calm demeanor veiled his own misgivings.

The hours crept by, and concerns for the boys' safety were suppressed as Tina and Sara carried on with their assigned jobs. They tried not to notice Maria and David's anxious looks at the road for signs of the boys' return.

Did the family hear an accusatory tone in Maria's voice when she spoke to David? "You're worried too, aren't you? They should have been home by now. I just knew we shouldn't have let them go by themselves."

Tina felt the familiar tightening in her chest as, for a moment, she let herself think her brothers might not be coming home. She put the thought down as she prayed the silent plea, "Please, Lord, bring our boys safely home."

David was determined to let nothing interfere with his work. His silence communicated itself to the rest of the family, as no one wanted to give voice to the unthinkable.

The sun had almost set when they heard the rattle of the wagon and the commotion of the travelers back in the barn. Their outbursts of joy and relief welcoming the boys back were quickly silenced when it became obvious that, although they were home, all had not gone well. The horse trembled with exertion and tossed its head in agitation. The wagon was mud-splattered and dragging dry branches and weeds.

The boys were inundated with questions, but Isaac just shook his head and busied himself with wiping down the sweating horse, while Cornelius began unhitching the wagon. Before they could give their anxious parents the details of their journey, from the bed of the wagon rose a ragged, filthy individual, his long beard matted and knotted with twigs and grass, his clothing a jumble of unrecognizable odds and ends. His pale face was contorted with pain. He held tightly to the sides of the cart and his body shook with frailty as he managed to step down to the floor. The pleading looks he shot David told of terror and dread. With obvious effort, he stood holding onto the mud-caked wagon's wheel.

Isaac seemed to have his agitation under control and was able to begin the story. "Papa, this man needs help. If it hadn't been for him, we might not be here now. On our way back home, two men were waiting for us on that piece of empty road outside of Halbstadt." His voice faltered. His deep breaths interrupted his attempts at continuing the tale.

Cornelius's voice was tight with fury as he took up the story. "One of them grabbed the horse's harness and the other one pushed us off the wagon. We fought hard to keep them away from us, but they were much better fighters than we were."

Isaac, with effort, recovered his equilibrium and tried to fill in the missing parts. "With this man's help we managed to beat them off and get away. We cut across the shallowest part of the river, and as they were on foot, we did manage to outrun them."

David eyed the man the boys had brought with them and saw he was in poor physical condition. His efforts at fighting off the thieves had cost him dearly, pushing him to the edge of collapse. Something about his dark eyes and rugged face looked oddly familiar.

"Come, I think you've used up all your energy in helping my sons. Tina, make a pot of tea with sugar, while your mother serves us all some of that soup we weren't hungry for during the day."

In the kitchen the man sank into the nearest chair and looked long and intently at David. "You don't remember me, do you?" he asked. "I think I've changed since the last time we saw each other."

David was startled by the statement and looked again at the unkempt individual occupying a chair in his kitchen. "Efim, is that you? Efim Golub? Is it really you? The last time we saw each other was the year after our wedding, when you gave the children all those goodies in your bakery. What has happened since then, and why are you wandering the countryside? What about your family and your store?"

"Where do I begin? It's all gone, the store, my family, my home . . . gone. It was the White Army, they hate us Jews just as much as the Reds or anyone else does. They took over the store and kicked us out of our home. We had nowhere to go except back to the Shtetl where my brother lives. He had very little for his own family, and certainly nothing to share with us."

Efim paused for long moments and wiped his face with a grimy cloth. His emaciated body was hunched and trembling when he carried on with his tale. "My wife died of typhus just after we got there, and my two sons were sick with the disease for months. I'm the only one able to work, so here I am. I'm still in business, only now I'm a peddler selling a few odds and ends to people who are just as poor as I am. I remembered the Mennonite colonies and thought someone might have a little food here, or a few rubles to share."

"Efim, our land is occupied by the German Army. We have four soldiers billeted here. They have been away for a few days, and only God knows when they'll be back. They will probably want to know who you are, so this might not be the best place for you, but you are welcome to stay as long as you need."

"Where *is* the best place, David?"

David shook his head in uncertainty and closed the door between the kitchen and the barn passageway. He pulled up a chair and placed his warm hand on the filthy sleeve of his old friend. "I can't thank you enough for what you did for my boys. For now, your best chance is here. You can share the boys' room in the barn, and you'll have to stay out of sight as much as you can. I doubt our four guests will be too concerned about your presence here, but you never know."

The family listened to Efim's story of theft, violence, rape and murder, one shared by so many. They were warned of the importance of keeping quiet about his presence. Increasingly their lives were full of secrets, omissions and fabrications, reluctantly practiced. Efim would have time to gain back some strength before continuing on his way.

Outwardly, conditions in the villages seemed almost normal. German protection meant fear of theft and home invasion receded. As spring progressed, the smell of moist fertile soil and budding branches filled the air. Plum, cherry, apricot, and apple trees bloomed in the warm spring sunshine. Gardens were planted, and potatoes, watermelons, carrots, cabbages and onions poked their leafy heads above the soil. Soon, the wheat and barley, looking hale and healthy, painted the rich black fields a luxuriant summer green. Some fields lay fallow, black voids reminding villagers of possible shortages of grain and cattle feed.

In the dark of an early summer night, loaded down with dried fruit and *zwieback*, Efim left his temporary refuge. After a hug for David and hearty handshakes with the boys and the rest of the family, he continued his search for a home. David watched him go and felt regret that there was not more he could do for him. No one but the family knew he had been there.

The *Selbstschutz* question still reverberated through villages and cities. The German occupiers were eager to provide training in weapons and in other military duties. For David Schroeder and other leaders of the community, the subject weighed heavily. The Penner relatives and other estate owners pressed hard for the institution of a trained militia, hoping for the return of some of the goods stolen from their homes.

Others agreed with David. "Is it not hypocritical to call ourselves nonresistant as long as our families are not in danger, yet we threaten to use weapons when we stand to lose our possessions?"

The question was to confound the Mennonite membership for many generations.

CHAPTER TWELVE

THE DRAGON OF WAR

Late 1918 – to Early 1919

BLUMENAU WAS FORTUNATE. THE NIGHTLY GUARDS HELD watch, and no serious confrontation occurred until near the middle of September, when a group of hungry peasants under cover of darkness broke into a granary and stole a few bags of wheat. The guards, as they had been taught, fired into the air causing the thieves to flee into the darkness, dropping two bags of grain. The gunfire caused tumult in the homes and precious hours of sleep were lost, but the village gave a collective sigh of relief that no one was injured. Other villages were not so lucky, as thieves and guards had been killed or injured.

The harvest had barely been brought in when new rumours began to fly. The anarchist Nestor Makhno was again beginning to flex his muscles. What should one believe about this controversial individual? Was he a devil in human shape, who slaughtered a family of five, beheaded them and set their heads around the kitchen table, or a progressive leader who instituted a new educational system in his home village? Was he an evil belligerent who hated Mennonites because of having been abused by one in an earlier place of employment? Was he a loving father with little children, or a lawless anarchist who lived by no other rule than his own?

The questions were set aside when, on November 11th, 1918, with the signing of the Armistice between the Allies and Germany, the war was over. Germany conceded defeat, and the occupied territories had to be vacated. With almost no warning, the German troops began leaving.

In the Schroeder household, with barely a word of good-by the four young billets packed up their belongings and by dawn had vacated their rooms.

An eerie silence settled over the villages. The protectors had gone and left the doors open. Who would enter?

"Why are all the windows and doors open?" asked Neta, shivering as she came into the kitchen the morning after they had left.

Tina pulled her shawl tighter and hurried to help her mother "Mama is airing out the house."

David smiled as he reminded his wife, "It's November! You will freeze us all out!"

Maria's wrinkled brow and tight lips warned her family to keep silent. She was on a cleaning rampage. "Boys," she called. "Bring in the water to heat. We will do a washing while the weather is still good enough to hang things outside to dry. I will not tolerate this smell one more day."

Maria's orders brought groans from all around. Tina and Sara had heard often enough, "the sooner begun, the sooner done," and wasted no time in collecting the clothing and bedding to be washed. Tina, being the oldest, did her part in making sure everyone helped.

"I hate wash day," moaned Sara.

"Who doesn't? But it's better to keep busy than to wonder and worry about what will happen next."

The cleaning rampage left them all exhausted, and after a supper of warmed-over sausage and noodles, they were happy just to rest and enjoy the solitude of their family home.

In the days following the German exit, their world held its breath. The sudden leaving of the troops had shocked everyone into wordless expectancy. What now? Who would come and what would they do?

Hardly a day had passed before reports of turmoil flew again. The anarchist, Nestor Makhno was again on the move, laying siege to villages on the northern edge of the Molotschna Colony. Terrified citizens were fleeing their homes. One day they heard the *Selbstschutz* forces were routing the invaders, the next they were being defeated. What to believe? Fear ruled the day.

Invaders again flooded the countryside as the destitute, hungry Russian peasants took what they felt belonged to them. To them the Mennonite villagers were the rich, the privileged, the greedy, the materialistic. The poor deserved better.

Meanwhile the fire-breathing dragon of war was growing a double head, aptly named Civil War.

CHAPTER THIRTEEN

LIVING OFF THE LAND

1919

ANOTHER NEW YEAR, ANOTHER PRAYER FOR PEACE WHILE CHAOS reigned. What would 1919 bring? What was the greatest threat, invasion by a hungry populace and anarchist bandits, or retribution from the Bolsheviks for what was seen as collaboration with the enemy? In the thirst for power, as one faction fought the other, would the welfare of the people be forgotten? Had it ever been considered?

In the Schroeder household, Sara was one of the first to experience the results of a civil war. The January chill had kept the families indoors, except to bring in fuel for the brick stove that straddled several rooms, keeping them all warm at once. Sara was in the back yard collecting the straw bundles for kindling when a shadow fell on the ground beside her. The first sound she heard was low mumbled voices, then the sight of five or six figures, adults, children, one bent and obviously elderly person.

She heard pleading words spoken in colloquial low-German, interspersed by stifled sobs and moans of pain.

David, coming to check on Sara's delay in bringing in the kindling, immediately recognized the group despite their attempts at concealing their identity. Without a single question he ushered them into the barn passageway out of the cold, and into the warmth of Maria's kitchen.

"Maria, it's my Uncle Peta and Aunt Selma from Memrik. They are on their way to the Crimea. They need a bed and some food."

Destitute was only one word to describe their plight. Hopeless they were, despondent, and miserable. "It was the bandits, there are so many coming and going it's hard to tell who they are. Our house was burned to the ground. We managed to save a few personal belongings, but other than that it's all gone. We have nothing. Selma has relations in the Crimea; it's our only hope."

Maria and Sara began the routine that was to become familiar for many months. Feed a hungry crowd, find them a bed, comfort the deserving, and tolerate the invaders.

The Russian villages lived on the edge of famine most every winter. The primary producers of food, the farmers, the grain growers, and the livestock tenders, through proper storage, were able to keep themselves fed and often donated extra food to the hungry cities.

With trepidation, farmers like David and Maria Schroeder eyed the emptying granaries. The family knew something was very wrong when David returned from a visit to the local Soviet, recently opened in the village. Never before had his family seen such a look of despair as he took his place at the table.

"David, what is it, what do they want now?" Maria's question could have been asked by any one of them. Visits to the Soviet never ended well.

Tina noticed how pale her Papa looked as he sat down and threw a notice on the table. The disorder and uncertainty were taking their toll.

"Another grain requisition, every farmer will be expected to deliver one more *pood* of wheat per *dessiatine*."

"Is there enough in the bin to cover that?" It was the question that would be asked in every household. What would be left for them after requisitions of grain, theft of flour and livestock, and shortages of animal fodder? Armies laughingly calling it "living off the land."

Scarcity fought with higher demand, leaving behind a deep cavern of need. The Triumvirate from hell was the White Army, the Red Army, and the Makhnovists, sawing back and forth across the "bread basket of Russia," plundering, destroying, and defiling.

CHAPTER FOURTEEN

SOMETHING FALLOW, SOMETHING FRUITFUL

February- June 1919

IN BLUMENAU, LIKE IN MOST MENNONITE VILLAGES, FAMILIES took care of each other. When one was in need, the others stepped in. The Penner relations were in need. The *Sommerfluss* estate had been ravaged first by government requisitions of land, grain and livestock, and then by roving bands of thieves. Bank accounts had been scavenged. The beautiful winter house in Halbstadt was occupied by others, Truda's carefully accumulated possessions damaged or destroyed.

Truda's sister, Hilda, needed a home. This intelligent young woman who wanted more from life than *Kinder, Kirche und Küche* (children, church, and kitchen) had chosen a radical path. Graduating from the Halbstadt Mennonite Mädchenschule and then the Kommerce Schule, she had made a bold move– nurses' training in a hospital in Switzerland.

During the war, nurses were in desperately short supply and Hilda and many other young women like her were conscripted into the Medical Corps under the auspices of the Red Cross.

Her tour of duty took her to the front lines, to face situations she could never have dreamt of. After three endless years with barely a rest, the young woman suffered a serious mental breakdown from the trauma of what she had seen, heard, and done. Silent, almost catatonic, she lived with images of pain and suffering while night terrors awoke her.

Truda Penner paid a desperate visit to her Schroeder cousins. They hardly recognized the formerly proud, full-bodied woman in charge of the *Sommerfluss* estate. She had become diminished, shrunken, her strident, commanding voice now hesitant and pleading.

"Maria, I've come to ask a huge favour. I am begging you to hear me out. I'm sure you have heard how our Hilda has suffered this last year. She can't survive this way much longer. Her mental state is the lowest it's ever been. What I'm asking is more than anyone has the right to ask, but I have no choice. Can you find it in your heart to give Hilda a home for a few weeks? We have no home left. She has nowhere to go."

Maria stood dumbfounded. "We have no medical knowledge. How could we possibly help? We have little left to give."

The woman's hands shook. Her lips trembled, and tears ran down her wasted cheeks. "I know what I'm asking is beyond anything one should be asked to give. We are trying to find a sanatorium for her. If you could just take her for a few weeks, we would be so grateful."

Maria was filled with dread at having the sick woman in her home, fearing her presence would be disturbing to the family, especially to Neta. It was Sara who pleaded her cause, promising to take over her care, "Mama, we can't let her go to some over-crowded hospital where she will just get worse and die. I will share whatever space we can find and take care of her."

When Maria saw the pale, silent woman she could not say no.

Though Hilda seemed unreachable at first, Sara was able to see what the others could not. Like the intrepid individual they had always known her to be, she took on the impossible task. Maria and David's misgivings at taking in such an ill person were calmed when they saw how easily Sara stepped into her role of caregiver.

David was amazed at his daughter's instinctive way of reaching through the curtain of fear and panic that separated Hilda from reality. "Sara seems to know exactly what to say and do. She just reaches out her hand and lets Hilda decide whether she will take it or not. She is so patient and loving. I have every hope it will all turn out well."

Sara spoke to Hilda as a little sister, telling her about the ordinary events in the household, the cow that had freshened, the neighbours who came to visit, the *zwieback* mother had made for *fesper* yesterday. Though the traumatized woman seemed not to hear a word, Sara carried on the one-sided conversation. She allowed no whisper of unwelcome news into the room.

No one spoke of the killings, the rapes, the destruction, the constant thievery or the massacre of a whole family in a village near Halbstadt.

She read to Hilda from the children's books her mother had read to her, told her the simple Bible stories from Sunday school, even though for many weeks Hilda's face did not change expression.

Over time, the words seemed to act like a lullaby and Hilda's night terrors lessened. Sara could often be heard singing the familiar church hymns she had grown up with and smiles lit the faces of the family, when one morning Hilda joined in.

A turning point had been reached. Slowly, after intermittent periods of regression and discouragement, Hilda's voice was heard in conversation, mainly with Sara but also with Neta, whose light-hearted chatter brought a smile back to a face that had forgotten how—a happy sign in a time of worry and fear.

Although Sara did her best to shelter Hilda's fragility from the mayhem and disorder that surrounded them, the rumours and warnings of danger insinuated themselves into the family's routine. Weeks of comparative peace and quiet were broken by hungry hordes breaking into the house, taking food or saleable items that could be traded.

Hilda was somewhat protected from the hordes. After one look at the staring eyes and skeletal frame of the distressed woman, thieves often backed out of the room, wanting nothing to do with a clearly mad woman.

As winter wore on, Hilda's health began to improve. She and Sara took on household chores, especially garden and yard work, enjoying the late winter briskness and sunshine as a reprieve from spending time indoors. Hilda still cringed at the sound of gunfire echoing from some distant skirmish, or the thunder of hooves drawing near to the village. Then she sat hidden in any dark corner she could find, her face in her hands, her shawl wrapped around herself, motionless and silent.

The villages suffered further incursions of the Red Army troops requisitioning grain, demanding meals, and searching the barns for useful livestock. Horses were in great demand. Weak, tired often sick animals were left behind.

No one would forget the day Cornelius watched in horror as his very own mare, pregnant with her first foal, was forced from her stall and beaten with leather thongs in the effort to tie her to the wagon carrying away the grain meant for planting.

His rage exploded as he saw the wild eyes looking to him for protection. "Stop! You can't take her! She's pregnant! She can't be run behind a wagon!" His outburst caught the thieves by surprise. Before they reacted, Cornelius began to untie the terrified animal.

"Now, now, little man," teased one of the soldiers. "We'll take good care of her. We are getting two for one. Now shut up and get out of here before we get rough with you."

Cornelius felt himself being grabbed from behind and pushed into a mound of rotting straw and manure. "Please, please, don't take her!" he pleaded.

"We said shut up. You asked for this!"

Cornelius braced himself for what he knew was coming. The pain of the kicks in his belly and groin made him scream in agony, no matter how he tried not to. The pain from one merged with another, and his abdomen felt like it was on fire. Finally, the kicks stopped but the pain raged on.

Someone had broken into the circle, someone wearing the red star-emblazoned cap, the belted uniform and the highly-polished black boots, someone in authority who with only one word put a stop to the misery. "Enough! Untie the horse! What do we want with a mare giving birth at any minute? You miserable louts!"

Cornelius felt pain in every bone of his body as he got to his feet. The company quieted down, but their glares told Cornelius it was just because they were obeying orders. Without any more words, they mounted up and were on their way.

With clenched fists and head held high, he watched them go. He felt like a child trying to hold back tears and it took some quivering deep breaths to regain control. He put his hand on the sweat-soaked back of the trembling mare and stood with her until her breathing slowed. The sight of the marks of the lashes on her back caused him as much agony as it did the horse.

He did what he could for the terrified animal, then hobbled down the long passageway to the kitchen, stopping every few steps to pull himself together and hide the signs of pain. Tina, busy at the kitchen stove could tell by the expression on her brother's face that something was wrong.

"What happened? Are you alright?"

"I'm fine."

Without another word and struggling to keep the limp out of his step, he headed to the room he shared with his brother. Tina knew better than to pursue him; her brothers were not ones to divulge their feelings.

It was not until Isaac noticed the bruises on his brother's body that the rest of the family heard what had happened. Losing a much-needed piece of livestock or seeing a pet injured felt like losing a family member. Many a farmer, with tears in his eyes, watched as a milk cow or necessary plough horse was led away. Any attempt to dissuade the marauders from taking the animals or the equipment was met with the slow and arrogant drawing of a weapon; once in a great while, mercy was shown.

Spring rains brought some weather relief. Gardens were planted. Fruit trees bloomed, and every edible product was preserved in whatever way worked best. Gooseberry soup was consumed with relish, even by the many who swore no single spoon of the tart mixture would ever pass their lips. The desperately important task of canning or pickling fruits and vegetables was left to the women, with more tasks to come when the season allowed.

David discussed the crop plans with Isaac and Cornelius, who were old enough to help not only with the work but with planning. "Boys, we have some decisions to make. There is only enough seed grain for less than half of what we normally plant."

Isaac had spoken to other farmers and had some ideas to share. "Papa, we can't leave fallow land. Something has to be planted."

Cornelius had read about suitable crops. "It will all depend on the seed we have. We can plant sunflowers; the Halbstadt manufacturers are building oil presses for producing vegetable oil for cooking and baking. We could also plant extra potatoes, onions and such, that way we still have a crop to sell."

David listened to the boys and added a few ideas of his own. "Watermelons are always in demand for pickling or for syrup. Now, if we have rainfall when it is needed, then we will still produce something."

Maria expressed the feelings of many. "If only the government would let us keep what we grow."

More and more was heard the disheartened response. "The more we grow, the more is taken."

David's mind whirled with the fears he discussed with Franz or other villagers but tried to keep from Maria. "There is a rumour going around that Makhno's band slaughtered sixteen people in Eichenfeld last week! That's less than a hundred kilometers from here. Will we have them here as well? Is it true the Red Army is executing anyone who has in any way opposed their regime? Could it include anyone who has been in the *Selbstschutz*? Is the White Army really back demanding food and lodging? Has nothing changed?"

Worries shared with someone who understood lightened the load. Franz Lentz often came in the evenings to sit on the front bench of the Schroeder's yard. "Have you heard the White army is asking for recruits of young men from our villages? Some have even volunteered. Some have simply been conscripted."

Just one more thing to worry about. Cornelius and Isaac were too young to join up, but how could he stop his seventeen-year-old stepson from doing something rash? At night, the problems were magnified, and for David a lack of sleep took its toll.

Isaac took his turn at guard duty. He had never joined a *Selbstschutz* unit feeling his place was on the farm with his parents and sisters. He remembered Franz's last words of advice to him, "Just concentrate on doing the work that needs to be done. You will be less likely to be injured if the gangs know you are unarmed. Let them take what they will. You can't do anything to stop them."

Fear, confusion, disagreement, helplessness or aggression, a mixture of emotions raged through homes and villages. More and more among families, the talk turned to the scarcity of food. When the rains came late, fewer *dessiatine* were planted, and with a shortage of work animals, it all bode badly for a bumper crop. More rumours were heard of famine in the Russian villages.

Every village was inundated with hungry families or children looking for food. Village councils felt something needed to be done about hungry children roaming the streets. Red Cross organizations were approached for help. The Blumenau Village Council heard suggestions from many individuals. Soup kitchens were suggested, but everyone knew the village could not provide meals for every hungry person who came to its door without help from aid organizations.

It was the women of the *Frauen Verein* who had a suggestion. "We can't help everyone. Our own families are doing without, but we can help some. If every village council contributes something, one central soup kitchen could be opened for families with small children."

Many suggestions were made and discarded until Sara and Hilda approached David and Maria with a timidly made suggestion. "We could open an orphanage."

"Open an orphanage! How could we possibly do that? We can hardly look after our own children, much less other people's."

The girls explained their much thought-out plan. "There are many empty houses that were abandoned when families moved, or elderly people died, so finding a home for the orphanage would be the easiest part. Every village in this district has money set aside for helping the poor. If every village contributed a specified amount it could be used to feed many children, and the Red Cross will contribute something, probably food. So many very little children come to our doors and how many of them die because they don't have families to help them? If the villages in our *volost* work together, we could raise enough money to open an orphanage for the very young."

David and Maria felt pride in the young women's ideas but were skeptical that the plan could work. "We'll have to think more about it and try to convince the councils that it would be possible." David had little hope but could not veto the plan without hurting the girl's feelings.

Maria and David discussed the possibilities. "I suspect Hilda is behind this idea," said Maria. "Her work with the Red Cross would have taught her something of what is needed in a children's home, and probably how to approach these organizations for help."

"Maria, do you think Hilda is well enough to take on such a huge job? She has barely recovered enough to function in our family. This job is more than taking care of children, it would mean finding food, clothing, and all the things children need. I don't know. It seems too much, too soon. Sara has no experience. We need to wait, give it some time and find out what the other villages think."

"I've seen how much work Hilda is doing in the house," continued Maria. "She's helping with getting meals on the table, and the family doesn't see how much of the cleaning is being done by her. She is an intelligent, hard-working woman. I am always surprised how she comes up with clever ideas about getting things done. I know her illness will cause some difficulties, but Sara is her best helper. If anyone can accomplish something like this, Sara and Hilda are the ones to do it."

There was an edge of impatience in David's voice. "Maria, how can two women find food, clothing, bedding and all the other things children need? I have to tell you, as much as I am afraid to say the words, that I see signs of food shortages everywhere I look. Our crops are half of what we expected. If we don't get more rain next year than what came this year, I am very afraid for what will happen."

Postponing the decision about the orphanage was all David could think of for the moment. "Let's wait and see what the other village councils say."

Meanwhile, Sara and Hilda made lists of necessities for a residence for fifteen children under the age of ten.

Maria saw the lines of worry etched in her beloved husband's face. In the stillness of the evening they often sat on the garden bench, taking comfort from the peace and quiet of the evening. Maria repeated the familiar words of assurance. "You know what we are told, over and over: God will take care of us. We have to have faith in Him."

"My heart says to have faith, but my head just says where was He when so many people in the colonies lost their lives at the hand of bandits last month? More than a hundred people, Maria. Where was God when those people needed help? Why should He help us?"

Never in their married life had David's voice sounded so despondent. For a long while David and Maria sat in downhearted silence. There were so many questions, and so few answers.

Like threads of black through a woven cloth ran the reports of villages laid waste and citizens murdered at the hand of the anarchist Makhno, whose forces seemed daily to be growing–25,000 they said, 50,000 or even 100,000 rebels.

CHAPTER FIFTEEN

MARAUDERS AT THE DOOR

Summer 1919

THE SEASON'S HEAT CARRIED ON. THEN, IN THE AFTERNOON OF one of the summer's hottest days, the skies darkened as huge dark clouds built up in the north, and flashes of lightening tore at the cloudy curtain, followed by the low rumble of thunder. A torrential downpour of rain lasted long enough to soak the arid fields and withering leaves, replacing worried looks with smiles of relief. The smell of moisture suggested a new vitality, and shouting children romped in the yards, letting the warm rain wash over them. Girls were usually not included in such rowdy behaviour, but the coming of the blessed rainstorms affected everyone.

The storm was scarcely over when the village experienced a storm of another kind. A cloud of dust and the thunder of hooves materialized into the sight of a band of about thirty riders on mud-spattered horses spreading through the village. It hadn't taken the marauders long to learn the element of surprise, in the invasion of a village, worked in their favour. The less time the citizens had to hide away goods, the more was available for pilfering.

The whole village felt the shock of noise, dirt and invasion. Terror-stricken children ran for the safety of their homes. Neta was one of them.

Never had she felt such relief as when the open front door of the house let her reach the safety of home. She collapsed against the wall of the small front room waiting for her pounding heart to return to normal. She had barely caught her breath when two individuals burst in behind her, filling the small entry way with the rank odor of wet clothing and unwashed bodies. They were stopped dead in their tracks at the sight of the young girl, long strands of wet hair hanging over her face and down the back of her wrinkled dress.

Her scream of terrified shock echoed through the house. *Flee, get away, run for safety;* but there was no safety, every avenue was blocked by the evil intruders. She stood defenseless, flattened against the wall, as far from them as she could get.

Hilda and Sara were in the back *kleinestubbe* working on plans for their project when they heard the commotion. Their first thought was for Neta. "Where is she?" With no consideration for their own safety, they ran towards the terrifying sounds of yelling and screams from the front of the house.

The men were frozen in the moment, staring in disbelief. Then, the grimy hands of one reached to stroke Neta's cheek. She shrank from the roughness of his fingers and shuddered at the closeness of his lips, wet with saliva and rain. A spray of muddy water from his hair hit the side of her face as he pressed closer.

"Such pretty hair, like gold. Your clothes are wet, we can help you get them off." Their words were almost unintelligible, but their lascivious stares needed no words.

At that moment Tina charged into the room. The sight of her little sister in the clutches of a vicious stranger sent a bolt of horror through her body. She pleaded, she begged, she prayed, "Let her go, she's only eleven. She's just a child. Please, please, leave her be."

The tallest of the two men held the young girl in a vice grip as she struggled and screamed. Never had Tina experienced such terror. She remembered Franz's comment about the gun or the ax. She knew she would use either one to save her little sister, if she had to.

In a blur of action rivaling her own, Hilda and Sara burst into the room. Hilda's skinny body, wild uncombed hair and sinewy arms presented a picture of menacing authority. "*Ostanovis!*" she shouted. "Stop!"

Her pale face was the embodiment of pure hatred and there was no sign of weakness or fear in her flashing eyes as she confronted the two individuals. Sara could only stare at her in amazement. Who was this person? The fragile being was gone and a bold, unflinching woman stood in her place.

Sara held her breath waiting for whatever violent reaction was bound to follow. The words she heard next were Hilda's. They were cold and dictatorial, a jumble of Russian words, unintelligible except to the two men who by now had lessened their grip on the child. Never had Hilda's voice taken on such authority. Her eyes blazed with a fury that matched the tone of the sentence she spoke.

"Let her go or you will carry forever the curse of the defiled."

The men hesitated momentarily but loosened their hold on the girl, as Hilda took from her pocket a small, cloth wrapped shape and, never taking her eyes off the pair, began unwrapping the silver crucifix it held. Pointing the crucifix at each of the men in turn, in a deadly quiet tone she began to speak, Russian words, sharp, clear, her eyes never leaving the faces of the two men.

With threatening steps in her direction, they spat out angry words, "Who do you think you are? You don't scare us!"

Hilda's face showed no sign of fear just the hint of a smile as she reached deeper into her pocket. "I might be a Mennonite, but I know how to use a weapon." There was pure shock on the men's faces as they saw in her hand a lady's gun, which at close range could be deadly. Her arm was steady, and her voice was strong. "Now get out of here and leave this girl alone!"

"You witch, you haven't seen the last of us. You won't always be here to protect her." In a last act of bravado, on their way out, they spat their venom of hate on the polished floor, leaving great gobs of mucus to mix with their muddy tacks.

Hilda marched out of the room as she un-cocked the weapon and placed it and the crucifix back into her pocket.

Tina and Sara were shaky with relief that it was over and could think only of the safety of their little sister. Tina led her to the comfort of the oven bench, held her close, and tried to calm her fears. Their tears mingled on the little girl's blanched face, while Tina whispered, "Shhh, you are safe. No one can hurt you now. We're here."

The two clung together, rocking back and forth until Neta's sobs subsided. Tina wondered how she would ever be able to let her sister out of her sight.

Neta's trauma was hard to overcome. Nothing could distract her from her experience until her parents came home and listened to the terrifying events. The thought of how close their youngest child had come to harm shook them to the core. With trembling voices, they thanked God, and praised Hilda's bravery.

David couldn't stop himself from checking every door and window over and over again to make sure they were locked, while Maria spent the night at the little girl's bedside.

Tina and Sara often wondered about the Russian words Hilda had said to the two men. She never spoke of the incident again, other than to assure the girls that her words carried no power, except to the men, who were not about to take a chance by ignoring them.

No one in the family asked Hilda if she would have shot the men to save Neta. They thought they knew. Maria shuddered to wonder where the weapon had been hidden during the period of Hilda's mental illness.

David only shook his head in amazement as he and Maria discussed the event later. "If Hilda can take on two brutes who are afraid of no one, she can probably get an orphanage built."

Part Three

WHEN ONE DOOR CLOSES

While place we seek, or place we shun
The soul finds happiness in none;
But with a God to guide our way,
'Tis equal joy, to go or stay.
Jeanne Marie Bouvier de la Motte 1648-1717

CHAPTER SIXTEEN

A HIDDEN DOORWAY

February 1920

TINA HELD THE SCOOP AND A BURLAP BAG AS DAVID SWEPT THE dusty floor of the barn attic. No kernel could be wasted. Wheat was precious, the staff of life, even if old and dusty, every kernel had the potential to produce hundreds more. They worked well together, as they always had. Although winter had not yet released its hold, David was anxious to begin preparation for the coming season. In a year when all was chaos and disorder, any routine was security.

David's steps were slower, his back bent, his face lined and serious. He didn't sing as he worked as he had when he first married her mother, enduring the laughter of the youngsters who had never heard their own father or anyone else's singing at work.

Around them, the walls of safety were crumbling. Neta's experience with the two ruffians had shaken them all. When doors allowed strangers in, threatening the wellbeing of their youngest child, it was hard to sleep at night. Visions of what could have happened tumbled around in their brains.

When every day brought the threat of some new affliction, the family clung to the ordinary, to the predictable. Coming in from their dusty work, David and Tina were greeted by the smell of the *zwieback* Maria had just taken from the kitchen side of the brick oven, to serve with the *borscht* soup she had prepared for lunch. Royal fare, even if the *zwieback* were less rich with butter and the *borscht* mostly cabbage.

Tina could hear the murmur of her parents' voices as she washed the itchy grain dust from her arms and hands. With sad news from every direction, small talk filled the time.

Maria had something positive to contribute. "I saw the two broody hens. It will be nice to have a few more chickens. Good thing the fields are bare of snow, they can find something to eat out there."

"Yes, I guess bare fields are good for something." Tina detected a note of impatience in David's voice.

She could tell her mother was trying to find a more uplifting topic of conversation. "I was just thinking; Isaac's birthday is coming. Maybe we can invite the family for *fesper* next week. It would be good to have everyone over for a visit."

David was having none of it. Every bit of news had its negative side, "Maria, don't forget, the Red Army is conscripting young Mennonite men now. Isaac could be one of them if this unpredictable bunch of reprobates thinks he should. You never know what to expect. I'm just glad he never joined the Selbstschutz–at least they can't say he was a traitor to his country."

It was easy to be discouraged when good news was so hard to come by. Maria was silenced by the reminder of Isaac being conscripted into the army. Tina knew by the long silences in her parents' conversation that stress was taking its toll.

The three sat at the table and joined in the simple grace that had been part of every meal as long as Tina could remember. "Come, Lord Jesus be our guest, and may this food to us be blessed."

David did have some positive news to contribute, "By the way, I was talking to Heinrich Thiessen the other day. The Village Council has been discussing opening an orphanage for Russian and Mennonite children."

Tina's attention was caught by the news, having listened to Sara and Hilda's endless discussions on the need for such a facility. "Sara and Hilda will be interested in hearing that. They're ready to take on the whole project if they can convince enough councilors."

A furrowed brow replaced Maria's placid expression as she passed a steaming bowl to her husband. Tina saw by David's quick look in his wife's direction that he knew, for Maria, this was upsetting news.

Maria expressed the thought each one of them had silently entertained. "How can they even think they can take on such a project?"

Mennonites generally found homes for their orphaned children among relatives and friends. Maria knew this home would be mostly for Russian children, the neediest, the starving, the neglected, often sick and close to death.

"Have they made any decisions about where it would be?"

"Nothing definite." David had related what he knew and now concentrated on the luxury of food on the table. "Maria, do we still have any of those bags of dried beans we had left over from the last few years?"

"I'm afraid only about half a bag is left. What are you thinking?"

"We have to find better places to store things. I am heartily sick and tired of having so much food stolen."

Hiding food, lean years, it all spoke of famine. Maria's shoulders sagged. "Where? Where won't they look?"

He patted her hand, "Don't worry, we will find someplace."

Tina heard confidence in his voice and for a moment the old adventuresome Papa she knew and loved returned. "You should ask Cornelius or Isaac; those two knew every hiding place in the house when we were young." Tina smiled as she remembered the games of hide-and-seek even her Boldt father would join in when they were children.

As the weeks passed by, Tina sensed neither David nor Maria were anxious to bring up the subject of opening an orphanage. April was nearly over when she saw Hilda and Sara, dressed in the few mismatched but presentable clothes they had left after thieves and marauders had taken their pick, leaving the house on a mission they were obviously not ready to discuss.

They were gone for the rest of the afternoon and even David was beginning to wonder where they could be. The family was sitting around the supper table and looked up in surprise when the two made an unusually exuberant entrance.

Hilda's complexion had lost some of its normal pallor, she stood taller and straighter, and her voice was more assertive, while Sara's cat-that-got-the-cream expression meant she had information she could hardly wait to relate. Tossing scarves and jackets on the nearest chair, they began to share their news.

"We have been to see Mr. Thiessen who is dealing with the need for an orphanage in this *volost*." Hilda took a deep breath and kept them all waiting as she got ready to tell the best part. "Eight villages in this district are contributing funds to set up a small orphanage, only about fifteen children for now, for young children under the age of ten."

While Hilda paused for breath, Sara rushed in to fill in the rest. "Hilda has been offered the position of manageress till permanent decisions are made."

So many questions—where, when, who else? Hilda's cheeks had taken on a hectic apple-red and her hands shook as she placed a sheaf of papers on the table. "Sara will be my helper for now, if she wants the position, and each village will provide workers in rotation as we get underway. The building they have in mind is the old Kroeker residence here in Blumenau, which was used as the old folks' home a few years ago."

Tina noticed her parents' silence and knew they had serious concerns about the venture. Was Hilda well enough to carry out the work involved? Could it be dangerous? Who would take over the girls' chores at home?

"Well, we will take this one step at a time." said David. "You two girls are smart and hardworking, and you'll have lots of help. This will mean so much to the children who need help."

Breaths were released as the two girls, having shared their news, let the overwhelming responsibility wash over them, relieved their parents were on their side.

David, as usual, gave them well thought-out advice. "Tomorrow we'll get the keys to the old Kroeker residence and you can begin deciding what is needed."

Sara smiled and nodded, pleased they had already set their papa's plan in motion. "We have the keys and were hoping you and Mama could come with us to give us suggestions."

Tina had her own doubts about the project. It seemed far beyond what two young women could take on. Who would pick up the pieces if the project ran into difficulty?

That night, again she had the dream that had interrupted her sleep several times in the last few weeks. Again, she stood on a hill, looking down into the gloomy mass of clouds gathered near the bottom. She dreaded going down the hill, yet something compelled her to take the first step, then another and another, down, down till she was running, faster and faster, the world a blur as she picked up speed, the momentum carrying her with breathtaking swiftness, finally crashing onto the rocky soil at the bottom of the hill. She woke with the pounding of her heart, wondering if she had shouted out her fear. No one stirred. Neta's breathing was still and regular, and Tina hardly moved, hoping that eventually sleep would return.

She woke later than usual, as sunshine poured into the room and sounds of breakfast cooking came from the kitchen. Neta was up, ready to have a sisterly chat while breakfast was cooking.

"Did you ever want to go to the *Mädchenschule* when you were my age?" Neta asked her sister.

To Tina it seemed too early in the morning to be discussing school of any kind, but especially the Girls' School in Halbstadt. "I guess I wasn't a very good student, not like you. All I wanted was to read books in my spare time. Plus, living with strangers scared me."

Neta agreed, "I wish the school was in Blumenau instead of Halbstadt. I'm not sure I want to live so far away from home either. I'd miss Mama and Papa, but Frieda and Suza are going, so at least I would have my friends with me."

Tina understood the idea of a boarding school could be quite attractive when all your friends were going. Six years in the *Dorfschule* was nothing, when compared to the years the girls from the estates spent, first with their local tutors, then at the *Mädchenschule* in Halbstadt, often quite far from their homes.

Tina understood her little sister's wishes but knew the cost of granting them would be huge. Higher taxes and larger grain requisitions left little for family expenses. Cost was secondary, anyway; the well-being of their daughter was her parents' first concern. Tina was quite sure her parents would never allow Neta to live so far away from home.

Neta still spoke of her encounter with the two ruffians in the front hall and seemed obsessed with finding safe places to hide. "If I'm ever outside alone, I'll make sure the door is locked behind me when I come and keep a lookout in case someone has followed me. I'll go straight to a hiding place and be very quiet, so no one will know where I am."

The memory of Neta's brush with calamity still caused an icy rush of fear to spread through Tina's chest. Her throat closed with dread as she watched her little sister carry on with her staunch determination never to be caught in such a situation again. Every day she breathed the same silent prayer, "Please, Lord, keep my little sister safe."

Neta was not the only one concerned with finding hiding places, not just for people but also for goods. Isaac spoke of the memory of a hidden doorway in the passageway leading to the barn. He questioned Tina as she cleaned out a closet, looking for any useful overlooked items.

"Don't you remember a small door in the wall under the attic stairs? It was too small for an adult to use, but we hid there when we played hide and seek."

"Isaac, I've been wracking my brains trying to remember what you're talking about. I just can't remember anything like that."

It was a spot that no one else seemed to remember, either. Was it some figment of Isaac's imagination? There was no door there now. Their mother was questioned but had little to offer. David had, of course, not been part of the family then.

It was their Uncle Kolya who finally added some useful information. "Your father did some work in the passageway near the stairs, if I remember right. The wall needed to be replaced because of dry rot or something. I helped him cover it with some boards left over from some other project. But Isaac, why would you remember that? You must have been no more than three or four at the time."

The memory of the doorway lingered in his mind but was pushed to the background when Hilda and Sara recruited him for endless chores in preparing the Blumenau Kinderheim for its opening in a few months.

CHAPTER SEVENTEEN

A BLANKET AND PILLOW FOR EVERY CHILD

1920

THE KINDERHEIM PROJECT BECAME EVERYONE'S PRIORITY.

As soon as it became obvious the undertaking was going ahead, every family member had time, ideas, and skills to contribute. It had taken almost four months of planning, wishing, hoping and endless back-breaking labor to get the building ready for use.

Gathering the materials to build the dormitory rooms with the plain shelf beds had not been difficult. Many times, a wagon would arrive, a young man would jump out, and Hilda or Sara would hear offers of help.

"We had these pieces of wood left from a building project. We thought maybe you could use them."

"I could help you build a few beds. I'm not too busy right now."

"Mother sent these clothes that my little brother outgrew. They have quite a few patches, but someone will be able to wear them."

Finding bedding was more difficult. So many goods had been stolen, damaged, or soiled. The ladies of the Frauen Verein came to the rescue. Every village had its group of talented women who created the quilted blankets so valued by anyone lucky enough to own one. From dark hiding places came bags of cloth scraps, too small for clothing–but sew enough of them together and you have a blanket.

These ladies seemed able to perform miracles. They washed, they mended, they stitched, knit and sewed. By the day of the opening, every bed had its straw-filled mattress, a sheet, pillow, and either one thick or two thin blankets. A stockpile of carefully mended dresses, shirts, jackets and underclothes filled empty cupboard drawers.

Despite a meager harvest because of little rainfall, food still appeared, delivered by handcarts or wagons from farther villages. Canned vegetables, dried fruit, smoked meats, sausages and *zwieback* baskets by the dozen. Every root cellar gave up something of its winter stock of carrots, potatoes, turnips, and cabbages. Every donated item was gratefully accepted and used to its full capacity.

When the donations ran out, would there be more coming? Would there be enough to feed families, let alone share with the needy? The mantra of the citizenry became, "If no one steals what we own, and the government lets us keep what we grow, we will survive."

August 1920

Even before the *Blumenau Kinderheim* (Children's Home) opened its doors, three children called it home. Two of them had been found in the Peters family's horse paddock on an August evening. One of them, a girl with tangled flaxen braids, was close to death from neglect and hunger. The other was a boy with a face so grimy as to be unrecognizable, wearing a tattered shirt which barely covered his swollen belly. Another child, a boy, with marks of trauma on his body, was in less danger of imminent death, but hid his face in the straw mattress or pillow and refused to look at or speak with anyone at the home. He ate only the smallest bits of food offered and hummed a tuneless melody until he fell into a restless sleep.

Hilda, as manageress decided which children to bring into the shelter of the Kinderheim. They had to be under the age of ten, without parents or siblings to watch over them, but Hilda knew making a choice between the needy would be difficult. Some would always touch the heart more than others.

Even with only three children, it became obvious that more help was needed. Hilda would be living at the Kinderheim, along with a rotation of young women from the eight district villages who would come to help with the work of keeping the orphanage open. Sara would come in every day, with Tina taking a turn on her sister's day off. There was enough money to pay everyone a minimal amount and to buy the food and medicine needed.

Hilda confided to Sara her plan for hiring extra help for the heavy work. "I think it would be a good idea to hire a Russian worker to tend to the heating, cleaning, and washing, and to take care of the cow and the horse. Maybe he could nurse poor old Blintzi back to health. Having even one carriage horse would be better than what we have now."

"Do you think you could find someone who is a hard worker, and honest and good with children, and on and on? My papa hasn't had good luck with Russian workers. They tend to come late, leave early, and are what he calls 'light-fingered.'"

Sara was surprised at Hilda's ready answer. "They are not all like that. I know a man from my time at the *Kommerce Schule*, I know that was a long time ago. He was the furnace keeper there, kept the place warm and clean, drove the wagon and carriage and tended the animals. He's kind and helpful and needs a job. Plus, he knows both Ukrainian and Russian and even some German, so he could help with translations."

If Sara had doubts about decisions made, she had learned to keep them to herself. "Well, hiring extra help sounds like a good plan. Just make sure this person is all the things you say he is."

Hilda responded with furrowed brow and tightened lips and Tina knew to say no more. The conversation was pushed to the back of her memory as the busy days before the opening of the Kinderheim absorbed her time.

Although the whole village had done their utmost, the Kinderheim still lacked some basic necessities. The coarse dark bags sewn by anyone who had time could hardly be called straw mattresses, as it was hard to find enough straw to fill them. In spite of all the efforts of the villages, three children, lucky to have a blanket and pillow, had to sleep with hastily-gathered bits of bedding covering the bunk's planks.

The family were concerned when they saw how exhausted and overworked Hilda was, those last few days before the opening. She was demanding more of herself than anyone asked. Every detail was tended to and nothing was good enough, causing her to become silent and depressed. Memories of her silent, uncommunicative months were hard to erase.

Sara and Tina tried to comfort Hilda the only way they knew. "Just think of where these children would be if they weren't here. It's not perfect, but at least they have someone who cares. It will get better."

On the day of the opening, families came to see the new venture and the renovated building. Curious, skinny, head-shaven children clustered together watching the visitors come and go. Sometimes, one would smile and assure their visitors that mother or father was coming to get them soon. So far, all the children were Russian and communicating was a problem, as accents and colloquialisms got in the way. However, a sad child rocked in the arms of a loving Oma, understood the song she sang no matter what the language.

At the end of the day, as the children slept in their beds, every worker, even Hilda, felt a sense of accomplishment for a job well done.

Hilda's unflagging energy became well known to everybody. The workers from the villages warned each other, "The slave-driver found more work for us to do. Now we have to change the sheets more often. My fingers will be raw if I have to wash one more sheet."

Sara understood their complaints. Hilda's almost obsessive need for cleanliness was well known, but not always understood.

The workers were told many times. "The children in our Kinderheim are so young, so fragile. We have to do everything in our power to keep them alive. Keeping them clean is the easiest thing we can do."

"If she was the one washing all those sheets, she might not think it was so easy." The workers grumbled at times but took pride in doing their best and were thrilled to see tiny bodies gaining strength and wan cheeks showing some colour.

Planning and preparing meals filled a large part of the day. Hilda's instructions were clear. "Breakfast has to be something filling. Oatmeal is best. Do we have any sugar? A tablespoon for each gives them a taste. Soup for the midday meal. Tante Loewen brought in a chicken whose laying days were over. What a treat that will be! Supper? Fried potatoes with a tablespoon of egg for everyone."

One day planned for, the next one waiting.

The Russian worker, Dimitri, was hired and everyone who knew him said he was skillful, kind and honest. Tina often discussed the worker situation with Sara. They had come to agree Hilda had made an excellent choice in hiring the tall, imposing individual whose dark Rasputin-like features took people aback when they first met him.

Sara was happy when she could go home to sleep. Staying at the Kinderheim with only a few workers and fifteen or more children carried a risk she preferred not to think about. Her encounter with two intruders in the hallway had happened months ago, but it still caused her sleepless nights, though she never let anyone know. Knowing Dimitri stayed every night was comforting.

With winter came darkness, discouragement, cold, more children, over-full beds, illnesses, coughing, crying, and even dying. Every hand was needed, every skill tested, every meal stretched to its limits.

When there wasn't enough help, death could focus its merciless gaze on a child and take it away almost before anyone noticed. Hilda and Sara seemed to be everywhere at once, but the endless demands on their time left them exhausted and discouraged. Tina's work at home was tiring, but it didn't suck the energy from her spirit the way Sara and Hilda's work at the orphanage seemed to do. Once or twice a week, Tina was asked to fill in for one of the exhausted girls from the villages.

The New Year brought new hope. How could 1921 be any worse than the previous years? As darkness gave way to light and winter drew to a close, the trill of a nightingale promised an early Ukrainian spring. Overwintered plants showed green in the garden. Neta joyfully brought in a few sprigs of lettuce which had survived the winter in the shelter of some other plant and shared them with the family.

In the orphanage, the children stretched arms and legs as warmth and sunshine filled the rooms. The workers were surprised when a sound unheard for quite some time echoed from one room to the next. It was the sound of laughter.

The village workers would take time from work to express their amazement. "There have been no more outbreaks of sickness for days now; hardly anyone is still coughing, every one of the children has been able to spend time outside. Even little Yuri is eating a bit more, and this morning he smiled at me and said he wanted more oatmeal. His sores have healed, and his bruises have finally disappeared."

Ukrainian summers could be scorching. This was one of them. The children spent time in the sun, and from receiving an amount of food many had never enjoyed in their whole lives, their cheeks showed some colour and the angular sharpness of their bodies some delicate curves.

Crops and pastures, orchards and gardens, all thrived in the spring abundance of warm weather and moisture. Rain came early then, as suddenly as it had come, it stopped as the coolness of spring gave way to the searing heat of summer.

Farmers warily eyed their fields. Were the leaves hanging more limply, more brown than green, even shriveled in places? Soon, everyone whose livelihood depended on the land--farmers, gardeners, cattlemen and horsemen -- were watching the sky for rain. Later, Tina often wondered how they survived that year of drought and knew that many didn't.

Franz Lentz, home on leave from his Red Cross duties, came to talk the situation over with David one evening, but saw Tina sitting alone on the garden bench under the drooping branches of the lilac hedge. Though they had known each other for years, they had rarely been alone together, and their conversation tended to be stilted and hesitant.

"Is it good to be home?" she asked.

"Nothing could be better than being at home."

Tina searched for a reply before the silence lasted too long. She was surprised to hear a tremble of emotion in his voice when he continued.

"I had no idea how much I would miss being at home, just seeing the fields and trees and feeling grass under my feet." After a tenuous silence, he carried on, "I hope you never have to spend time in the city, Tina. Nothing grows. The ground is covered with filth. You can't breathe. In the city, people are dying like flies. Everywhere you look, all you see is people begging for some little crumb of food."

Tina was horrified, by what she was hearing and fearful of what might follow. She had never before seen such an expression of despondency on the face of her jovial, confident neighbour.

"You have to walk around dead bodies lying on the streets and platforms of train stations. These people must have died trying to find somewhere to go, anywhere there might be food."

Franz covered his face with a shaking hand before he continued.

"I saw things I would never have thought I would have to see, even in my wildest dreams. Bone-thin, starving children desperate for even the tiniest crumb of food. I have heard that people eat dogs and cats . . . and God help us, even each other. What is happening there is beyond belief. How has our country sunk so low that our leaders walk away, like those children are nothing?"

Tina could never remember what impulse made her reach to cover Franz's clenched hands with her own. She just knew the clasp of those warm strong fingers helped her see something she had never seen before. They sat in silence while Franz struggled to gain control of his feelings.

"I had no idea how horrible it was." Tina knew they were empty words, meaning nothing, yet they seemed to bring them both some sense of consolation.

Franz held the touch for several moments longer until propriety won over emotion. Unengaged couples didn't sit together, holding hands in public.

Franz stood to take his leave. "I'm sorry, I'm not good company tonight. I had no intention of pouring all this misery out on you." He squeezed her hand and rose to head back to the opening in the hedge that took him home.

She sat for a while on the garden bench, shaken at the picture Franz had painted for her. Children lying dead in the streets? How could a country known for its fertile fields of grain allow children to die of starvation, their skeletal bodies lying discarded and forgotten? What if no more rain came? What if the crops were again diminished by drought? Would famine be their lot, too? Was the Bread Basket of Russia almost empty?

There were so many unanswerable questions, but one thing Tina knew was that her hand would always be ready when Franz needed someone to cling to.

CHAPTER EIGHTEEN

SOMEONE ELSE'S CHILD

Spring 1921

TINA BREATHED IN THE EARLY MORNING AIR, CLEAN AND COOL like the sheets she was hanging on the line. It gave her a moment of enjoyment in the midst of the drudgery of washday at the Kinderheim.

She later wondered what made her notice the boy under the willow bushes. He sat so still. Maybe that was what had caught her eye, his total stillness. For a moment she had the dreadful feeling he was dead, but then he raised his head and his woeful, dark eyes met hers. She wanted to look away, shutting out that accusing stare that told her, *don't just stand there, do something*.

She wanted to tell the boy, "I don't belong here. I'm just filling in for someone who couldn't come. The only reason my hands are clean is because I've spent the last hour washing sheets. I've been here all night, cleaning up after sick children, I stink of vomit and poop and I just can't handle one more sad story, beside which, you are too old for this place. I can't help you."

That was when another head appeared, like a small ghost, a finely shaped skull, darkly feathered in the early morning light. What she saw stunned her. On that ravaged little face was a smile. It hit her like a blow. There was nothing to smile about, yet there it was, the tremulous pleading smile that begged, *please, help me.*

They looked to be brothers, both with the pale sculpted cheeks of the starving. The little boy's head sank onto his brother's shoulder, going back to sleep, a faint smile still on his face.

Of all the things she felt like saying, what came out was, "What is the little boy's name? He doesn't look well."

"He's Ivan . . . my brother. I'm Symon. My sister Iryna died in the nuns' orphanage. I don't know where to go." A gut-wrenching sob shook his body. Tina held her breath while wondering if the boy would ever take another one.

Two more children, abandoned, sick, hungry, maybe near death. Two more out of hundreds, thousands. Why were these different from the rest?

The Kinderheim was full. Tina knew bringing these two in to face Hilda, who had already squeezed the last inch of space from the makeshift surroundings, might be useless. Like taking the step down the hill in her dream, she was compelled to extend her hand to the boy. He clutched at it, pulling himself to his feet, then turned to help his little brother. Tina saw there was no alternative but to lift the little one to standing, her hands encircling the fragile, stick-like bones of his back and ribs.

Leaving her laundry basket behind, she led the two into the over-crowded Kinderheim.

There was no turning back. The future hinged on a boy's smile, his brother's tears, and on the benevolence of two single-minded young women.

Tina led the way inside and into the tiny room Hilda used for an office. She wanted to lift the smaller boy but resisted holding the little body close to her wet, smelly garments. The older boy followed close behind, occasional sobs still convulsing his body. They found Hilda at her desk, surrounded by paper-work.

"Hilda, I'm sorry for the interruption, but I'm not sure what to do. This little fellow is in very poor condition, he needs help now."

Hilda's head fell forward onto her propped-up hand. Another child on the edge of the abyss! She had no tears left for hungry and abandoned children, but she gave a huge sigh of resignation and Tina knew she had won. "If you can find a place for him to sleep, then I guess the little one can stay."

Tina, with false bravado announced, "There's always room for one more."

Hilda had heard all the platitudes, the words of encouragement. "Tell that to the orphanage committee, they won't be happy with what we are doing. The little boy can stay, he's almost at the end of his rope, but the older boy will have to go elsewhere. What about food, is there always food for one more, too?"

"Yes," said Tina, "for these two there will always be enough."

Hilda had seen the signs many times and had often uttered her solemn words of warning, to which no one ever listened. "Never fall in love with someone else's child."

A bed was found for Ivan only because Tante Lentz had brought in a freshly laundered mattress bag, vacated by another wasted little body that would no longer be needing it. Symon was allowed to stay for the night and shared the bed with Ivan, whose fingers could not be pried from his brother's shirt.

Dimitri had taken on the job of bathing the grimy little boy patients and washing their hardly-recognizable clothing. It was Dmitri who discovered, in a ragged pocket of Ivan's shirt, the rusty little toy truck, left over from better days. Symon had his own treasure from the past hidden in his trouser pocket, a barely-visible, much-folded picture of a young couple on the day of their wedding. Dimitri wrapped the two small treasures in a clean scrap of cloth and slipped them into his own pocket.

With food in their bellies, in clean underclothes, tucked into what came as close to a real bed as they had experienced for many days, the exhausted boys slept.

Sara came in later that afternoon to take her turn at filling in for missing workers. Tina told her of the two fledgling sparrows she had found fallen from their willow-tree nest. It was Sara who heard the heart-broken sobbing of one of them after Ivan discovered his truck was missing. His garbled mixture of sobbing and colloquial Ukrainian was easier to understand than the sullen stare of his brother, who held onto the child but said not a word. When she finally understood Ivan's explanation for his wailing, she knew Hilda would have to be informed. After all, it was Dimitri who looked after the two boys' clothing when they came in, and he would have found the missing objects.

Sara found Hilda in the kitchen area. Her pencil and paper were out as she recorded the food available and planned the meals that would feed the most children.

"Hilda, there is something I have to tell you. Dimitri was the one who cleaned up the boys' clothing. Now something is missing, and the little boy is very upset."

"And you think Dimitri stole the items to sell, don't you?" Hilda's look was as accusatory as Symon's.

Sara was taken aback by Hilda's quick response. "What else can I think? He was the last to see them, and now they're gone."

"Maybe instead of making accusations you could have asked him about them." Hilda's angry expression reminded Sara of the day in the hallway and the cold-eyed look Hilda had given the intruders.

Before anything more could be said, Hilda pulled the items from her pocket. "There, Dimitri gave them to me, a little toy truck and a wedding picture. I was just waiting until the boys woke up to return them."

Sara's apology was too little, too late, as properly chastened she watched Hilda march from the room. Yet something puzzled her. Why would Hilda be so angry?

Worrying about small mysteries had no place in the crowded days of tending sick children, of trying to find food to fill hungry bellies, and keeping up even a minimum standard of cleanliness.

Another problem needed solving. Symon's single night at the Kinderheim had quietly been extended as no one had the heart to tell young Ivan that his brother would no longer be living with him.

Sara hoped Hilda had forgotten about the situation, but Hilda rarely forgot anything. "He's more than ten. The Kinderheim Committee will not increase our funds for an older child when we are already over-crowded."

Sara's crestfallen look brightened when Hilda conceded, "He can stay as long as the cool weather holds, but when summer comes, he will have to find another place."

Summer 1921

Summer warmth lifted spirits. No one said anything about Symon's leaving and Sara was glad not to ask any questions. Both in the Kinderheim and in the village, children reveled in the freedom of July, spending as much time outdoors as possible. In the villages anxious adults watched the cloudless skies for signs of rain. Instead of rain, what they often saw was the impassive face of a messenger from the Village Soviet, bringing another dreaded requisition notice. More grain was needed for government coffers.

Grain fields withered, and gardens hung limp and pale. Because Sara spent so much time at the Kinderheim, Tina and Neta were elected for garden duty. How much easier it would have been if only it would rain. Letting the stunted plants die was not an option, and everyone pitched in when they could. The water nature refused to provide had to be delivered by people.

"What are we watering today?" asked Neta as she trudged up the slope with two small buckets of water from the Kuruschan River, which divided their property.

Tina's buckets were larger, the path seemed further. "The potatoes again. Just a few more trips for now, then the cabbages."

Everyone's work was strenuous and backbreaking in its own way. Cornelius and Isaac took on the field work, cutting whatever hay had grown tall enough to cut, storing it in the barn attic, sharpening the scythe for the grain cutter, and finding and fixing parts just in case there was any grain to harvest.

Maria filled every jar she could find with fruit preserves and dried the shrunken plums, cherries and apricots for the delicious fruit compote, pluma moos, for a special *fesper*.

The field work was left to the boys and sometimes hired workers, but Tina and Neta were determined to help where they could. Harvesting wheat meant setting up the grain bundles for drying and threshing, something even Neta could do, especially in a year of sparse yield.

Although the bundles were not too heavy, after hours of plodding through the sharp stubble of the grain fields their legs burned from the scratches left by the sharp ends of the cut stalks of wheat. Tina swished her skirts back and forth trying to cool the burning pain and Neta followed suit, but the relief was only momentary.

If the field work was hot and dirty, Cornelius was equally hot in the shed where the wheat bundles were flailed with discriminating care, making sure every single grain was collected ready for grinding. Cornelius reminisced about the steam-powered grain-separating machines that had been used communally before the revolution. The huge steam engine the village owned had been out of order for several years. The agricultural industry was low in the order of needs for fuel and repairs. War munitions were first in line, yet every kernel of wheat was seized by the government.

The Peters' mill on the Kuruschan River was at a standstill due to broken parts. It meant the grain had to be hauled an extra seven *verst* there and back, to another mill to be ground into flour. Harvesting took more time and strenuous labour with little to show for it. Isaac was using Tanta Lentz's team and wagon to haul her and his papa's grain the longer distance to the mill on the Molotschna River.

For the fourth time this season, another requisition notice was posted at the Blumenau Council office. How much this time? Isaac and Cornelius watched as their Papa read the newly-arrived notice and saw how the furrowed frown was becoming engraved on his usually sunny features.

At supper that night David told the family he had heard the Penner relatives had to yield all the grain they harvested to the government by way of requisition this year.

"They managed to accumulate enough seed to plant about half of the piece of land they still owned. The rest belonged to new Russian owners who had less equipment and even less experience. Yesterday, Penner received a tax notice requiring two pood of grain for each dessiatine of the five hundred they had once owned. They tried to tell the tax collector four hundred dessiatine of the piece they once owned now belonged to someone else and got nothing but shoulder shrugs and bored looks. It will mean almost all the grain they have harvested will have to be delivered as the tax requisition."

In a rare show of anger, David crumpled the notice he had received from the Village Council into a ball and threw it across the room. No one said anything as he pushed his chair away from the table and left the room. What was there to say?

All Isaac could talk about was finding ways to hide whatever grain they could, leaving less for the grain collectors to find. Cornelius and Tina exchanged glances when they heard of his often-repeated ideas but said nothing. It seemed like just some wild notion by a young man grasping at straws, even though he knew hiding grain from the collectors was a criminal offense.

David was not the only one with unwelcome news.

Bad news traveled fast, and Maria was often the one to bring the sad tales to her family. After so many woeful stories, the fountain of her tears seemed to have dried up and her face often took on the blankness of despair. "You remember my friend, Mariechen Enns from Gnadentahl? Her two boys, Johann and Willy, died from typhus last week, and yesterday she died as well. Four other children are left without a mother. How can God let this happen?"

The family had no words of consolation; they had been repeated so often they lost all meaning.

There was anger mixed with sorrow in Maria's voice. "Have we not had enough grief? Typhus, diphtheria, whooping cough! That's all we hear, people dying. Last week, six people in Schoensee died! How much more can we take?"

Neta was too young to remember other outbreaks of illness. "What is typhus? Can we catch it?"

Maria tried to explain the dread disease without adding more fear to the situation. "It makes people very sick with headaches, a fever, and a rash. It's spread by lice. We don't have lice in our house, so you don't have to worry about that."

"Where do the lice come from?"

Maria was reluctant to go into detail about the spread of lice, but it was well known that marauding bandits and gangs were carriers of the virulent pests and left behind both the insects and the disease.

Neta didn't notice her mother's hesitation, and worried mostly about her own risk of coming down with the deadly disease. "Do you think the people in Schoensee had lice?

"Well, they must have."

"Can children get it?"

"Yes, it's possible." Maria patted her daughter's hand and gave the easy answer, the standard answer, the comforting answer. "The Lord Jesus has protected us, and we have to thank Him and pray that He will protect us now too."

It satisfied Neta. Tina and Sara exchanged glances. What about all the hundreds who had died in the villages over the last five years or more? Who had protected them? Was it faithless even to entertain the question? Why should God protect this family when so many others lost loved ones?

Illness was not the only peril they faced. Despite all the watering with buckets and barrels, gardens had yielded little. Fruit trees, generally an easy source of food, produced shrunken plums, cherries and pears, too little to do anything with other than to dry. Every family member guarded the meagre results of the garden. Potatoes were small and scabby, carrots twisted and hardly big enough to be pulled from the ground. Beans were used up as fresh or saved for drying. Every bit was precious.

Meals were made from the least produce possible to feed the most people. Any garden vegetable too small to cook on its own was added to stews or soup, and chicken soup was served with an extra ration of noodles.

The family ate without the usual hearty appetite. The silent meal, everyone preoccupied with their own thoughts was becoming more common. Could more suffering possibly be borne? Apparently, the answer was yes.

On November 15th, a notice was posted on a Blumenau Council notice board. The lengthy list of names contained three from Blumenau. Isaac didn't need to read it to know his name was on it. He was the right age. In one month, on December 15th, he and two others would be officially conscripted into the Red Army.

When Maria heard the news, she busied herself in the kitchen before Isaac could see the tears she fought to hold back. Getting a meal on the table was the first thing to deal with. Grieving for her son, for herself, and the other mothers who were receiving the same message would be confined to the privacy of her own room.

Isaac said nothing on the subject, which was barely alluded to as the day went by. No one wanted to broach it and the meal passed in awkward silence or meaningless chatter.

Cornelius and Tina kept an eye on their brother. After the meal was over, he stood in the passageway between the kitchen and the storage barn, lost in thought. In the old European style, the kitchen of the house was attached to the barn and storage area by a long walkway lined with hooks and shelves for off-season clothing and household necessities. A staircase led to the attic area above the barn.

In the last two months, bandits had broken into the storage barn three times and stolen jars of canned vegetables, clothing, dried fruit and bags of flour. Soon there would be nothing left. Was there a way to create a storage area hidden to them?

Cornelius watched his brother until curiosity got the better of him. "What are you looking at? You've been standing here forever just staring at the wall. Are you alright?"

Isaac shook his head, "I remember as a child seeing a door in the wall under the staircase. Was I dreaming? You don't remember anything like that?"

Cornelius looked at his brother incredulously. "No. You must have been dreaming if you thought there was a doorway here. It's a solid wall. No sign of a door here."

Isaac stood tapping the palm of his hand with a woodworking pencil he had pulled from his pocket. "There is empty space under the staircase; we have to make use of it somehow. If there is no doorway, we are going to make one. It will need to look the same as it does now. Even a small storage area would help. We need to remove these boards one at a time, making sure we don't destroy any of the wood."

Cornelius shrugged his shoulders, "I still think you're dreaming, but I'll do what I can."

The project was on. The family was willing to let Isaac carry on, if for no other reason than to help take his mind off his coming conscription. It had to be done in total secrecy and not a single board broken, or one nail lost, to hide all evidence of work done.

Day by day, the top layer of boards was removed, exposing behind it another poorly-constructed wall, made of rough, splintery wood. The work was tedious and time-consuming.

Cornelius used his claw hammer with particular care to pull one last nail from a board. "I don't believe it! There's empty space under this board, like something has been cut away! I can see into the space under the stairs. Let's get these last few boards off!"

Encouraged by what they had found, the two worked to remove the top layer of boards. There at the narrower end of the wall they saw it, an opening, something a three or four-year-old child might call a door.

Cornelius gave a shout of delight and held up the coal-oil lamp used to light the passageway. In its dim light they could see that the empty space under the stairs was not empty at all.

"Call the others, tell them we found something," said Isaac, taking the lamp from his brother and peering into the darkness inside the opening.

With dubious curiosity the family made their way into the wood-strewn area. What could possibly have been found?

Maria was the first to arrive, noticing only the pile of scrap wood. "What have you done? What a mess!"

It was only after Isaac brought the lamp closer to the opening that Maria began to take it all in. "What is this? Where did this come from? There are sacks in there! Burlap sacks, full of something!"

Neta bounced up and down in excitement as she surveyed the scene, "Maybe they are full of gold! Maybe we are rich!"

David and Isaac pulled a bag from its hiding place while Maria and the others crowded around. "Something better than gold. It's wheat, sacks of grain! It looks like five or six and quite a few bags of something else." The smaller bags were found to contain dried beans, apples, prunes and rice. Stunned and disbelieving, the family stood by in astonishment at this amazing stroke of good fortune.

Maria, still in disbelief, told her children what she could remember of work their father had done on the buildings when they were young. "Your father was always building something, improving the barn and shed. I didn't pay too much attention. I do remember him telling you children the Bible story of Joseph storing food from the good years for use during the lean years."

A light went on for Tina, "I remember that! I loved that story! I asked him to tell it over and over. That's what he must have been doing, storing food for the lean years."

Maria smiled and shook her head, still amazed at what had happened. "Maybe he thought it was something he could do for his family in case they were ever in need. If he ever told me what he was doing, I've forgotten all about it."

Smiles mingled with tears as the family examined the contents of the secret storeroom.

"Isaac, how do you remember seeing him work on this?" asked Tina.

"All I remember is being small enough to walk back and forth through the opening. I guess to me it was a door." Isaac stood staring at the space as if it might disappear if he took his eyes from it.

David shook his head as he viewed the miracle. "What do we do now? This must be the deepest secret between us. No one, not your parents, Maria, or your brothers or sisters can be told. Sara is the only other person who can know about this. If word gets out, we could be in serious trouble!" No one wanted to get caught committing the crime of storing grain for their family's use.

Maria was already planning on how to fill the bit of empty space left with dried beans and fruit, and the few jars of canned vegetables left after looters had carried everything away.

The bigger problem was how to access the goods without revealing their hiding place. David and his two stepsons already had their heads together, testing ways to accomplish this.

The boys regaled their siblings with the story of the discovery.

"I was ready to give up," said Cornelius, "but the slave-driver here wouldn't hear of it."

"Good thing, too. We would never have found it if I had listened to all of you." Isaac's normally taciturn face held a broad smile.

Neta spoke for all of them as she gave her brother an unexpected hug, "You were right, and we were wrong. Thank-you, thank-you." The discovery had softened the impending dread of Isaac's departure.

The pages on Maria's devotional calendar dwindled as the count-down to Isaac's departure began. Maria used some of the dried apples and prunes to make perishky and platz for a special farewell *fesper* on the day before his departure. No one wanted to call it that.

Cornelius teased, "Finally, I will have the whole bed to myself."

The girls joined in the charade, " . . . and we won't have so many muddy foot prints to clean up."

Isaac tried to act bravely unconcerned, while Maria and David concentrated on looking ahead to his return. Mennonite emotions were kept in check, their feelings though keenly felt were masked by silence and stoicism.

The goodbyes were said at home, with all the girls, including Hilda, watching as the *droschke* driven by Dimitri, was readied for the trip to the Lichtenau train station. David and Maria would accompany Isaac there to meet his service brothers, while the others would stay at home trying to fill the hours with mundane chores.

When the clip-clop of the horses' hooves faded into the distance, Sara and Hilda went back to the Kinderheim, to the endless chores and children who waited for them. There was no time for loneliness or worry for their brother.

At the Kinderheim Ivan greeted them both like long lost family. Even Symon, whose presence had become so familiar no one questioned it, welcomed them in his own taciturn way. Daily food, even small amounts, had worked wonders on Ivan's skeletal little face. His cheeks had filled out, his eyes were no longer sunken and dull, and the haunted look was replaced by tentative smiles. He followed Sara around like a shadow, "helping" when he could. Tina visited when she filled in for other workers and the little boy adopted her as well. She brought tiny treats for him, after demanding cross-your-heart promises not to tell anyone.

David and Maria visited other family on their way home from seeing Isaac off. Tina tried to fill in for them, keeping Neta from feeling lonely and Cornelius from despondence as the world around them began to slump into famine.

Evenings for sitting on the garden bench were drawing to a close. Franz came to visit with Cornelius, and occasionally Tina sat at the kitchen table with them as they discussed the situation of their country and the Molotschna Colony villages. Cornelius soon lost interest in political discussions, leaving Franz and Tina alone to discuss the threatening future. Sara and Neta joined them at times and laughter and stories lightened the mood.

CHAPTER NINETEEN

JUST A LITTLE BITE

January 1922

CHRISTMAS PREPARATIONS AWAITED MARIA AND DAVID AT home after a short visit with relatives in Lichtenau. The Christmas meals would hardly resemble those from years past, and although Maria could think only about Isaac's absence, she did her best. She was determined to share the joy of their treasure with others while keeping in mind the necessity for secrecy.

"There is too much hunger in our country to celebrate like we used to. The Kinderheim needs food, and so many families have much less than we have. Sharing is part of our duty as Christians."

Maria worked her magic and sent vegetables and dried fruit to the Kinderheim, and small packets of beans or grain to families in dire need. Though some came from the hidden treasure under the stairs, she was mindful of what must last until the next crop year.

So far, the tiny doorway was covered by clothes hooks and shelves, revealing nothing of what lay underneath. Access took careful work, as Cornelius and David allowed plenty of time for every board and nail to be removed without leaving a sign behind.

The New Year at the Kinderheim started with a more abundant celebration than most of the children had experienced in a lifetime.

Ivan's sunny disposition shone through and he grinned with pure joy when either Sara or Tina came to visit or work. He made up for Symon's continued dark scowls and curt comments. Although Symon continued to sleep at the orphanage, on warmer days he spent his time wandering the countryside with a gang of friends, finding food or the odd item to trade or sell. He found an almost daily meal at one of the soup kitchens set up in some of the Russian villages. One meal a day -- it was something to count on.

Symon had found a place to hide his parents' wedding picture and Ivan's truck. Every now and then, the two boys took their treasures out of the nook in the back of a closet and examined them carefully, almost as if they had never seen them before. Symon always seemed to have lots to say to his little brother on such occasions.

Tina began to be concerned when Ivan excitedly reported his brother's promises to him. "Symon says one of these days we are going to go home," he said. "Our mother might have come home and will be waiting for us. We'll go see Vasily and Marya, and they'll tell her we're home."

"Who are Vasily and Marya?" asked Tina.

She realized how little Ivan remembered when he hesitated before he answered, "They are some people Symon knows."

"Do you remember your mother, Ivan?" Tina inquired, and felt nothing but grief when he answered.

"I remember Iryna. She was my sister. She got sick and died at the orphanage. I miss her."

Her arms encircled the wiry little body when she remembered Hilda's adage. "Never fall in love with someone else's child." It was too late.

Symon often reminded his brother of the important things in his life. "Do you remember who gave you the truck?"

"My father, Orst Danilenko gave me the truck. My mother, Sophia and my sister Iryna and my brother Symon are my family." Ivan recited the words Symon had practiced with him. He never thought about why it was important to remember those names. Tina and Sara were the names he used now, and Hilda.

To Ivan, like all the children at the Kinderheim, having food on the table and a place to sleep was what was important. Safety was not something they thought of. They heard sounds and shouting voices in the night, but signs of danger had become meaningless to them. Sometimes people would come into their room, strangers, usually shooed out by one of the workers. Why were they there? Sometimes they took things that did not belong to them, and Dimitri made them give them back. In the morning they heard the workers talking about what had happened.

"Good thing Dimitri was there. He's so big and strong, thieves are afraid of him."

For the children, Hilda and Dimitri were the bosses, respected and obeyed. For friendship and kindness, they turned to Sara and Tina. Tina tried to explain to the children that Hilda and Dimitri had a lot of work to do to keep the Kinderheim running smoothly, so they didn't always have time to visit or chat.

Stunted crops yielded only meagre amounts of grain, far less than was needed to feed the hungry masses. Tina spent more and more time at the Kinderheim filling in for workers who, due to the lack of food, had become ill or too weak to work.

Hilda did have some good news. A package wrapped in brown paper found its way to the orphanage door one chilly morning in February. Some of the children saw it arrive and gathered around, demanding to see its contents. Carefully, she removed each sheet of paper as the children watched with hungry eyes.

"What is it? What is it?"

Were they disappointed to see packages of rice, dried herring, beans and dried fruit, or did they realize a relief agency in Canada had just sent them the gift of life?

More soup kitchens sprang up, and the hungry and home-less congregated there and at train stations, probably hoping the trains could take them somewhere, anywhere there was food. Stories of dying children reduced to eating rotting flesh of animals and decomposed vegetables, grasses, mice and rats spread over the countryside.

Like a storm, the famine swept through the land. In the Schroeder household the carefully-guarded stores diminished day by day. Sara spent most of her time at the Kinderheim helping to stretch the food so every child would have something to eat. At home, Tina and her mama worked hard to produce at least one nourishing meal a day for as many mouths as possible. Pleas for help from starving relatives cast a pall over their home. How many could they possibly help?

For Tina, the ultimate pain was seeing Neta's thin arms and her face take on the sculpted look of a porcelain doll, and Cornelius's husky body shrink to manikin size. Her parents aged almost overnight, her mama's wrinkled arms and legs looking hardly strong enough to support her weight, while her papa's frame seemed to be folding in on itself.

She and Sara tried to find humour in the fact that their own clothing hung so loosely on them. "We look like a pair of scarecrows," laughed Sara, but Tina noticed when her sister looked in the mirror her eyes welled up with tears.

The nadir came in the final days of March, when only a half bag of wheat remained in the hidden pantry.

"You know we have to keep enough for seed." When she saw the tears in her papa's eyes as he tried to make his family understand how important it was to know a crop would be planted, keeping hope for the future alive, Tina's heart broke.

Many owed their lives to the distribution of dried beans, rice and herring from the Mennonite Central Committee in America and the soup kitchens operated by the American Relief Agency. Parcels of food also arrived from Canadian and American relatives. Churches and synagogues continued to pour aid into their starving country. In spite of the good will of so many, hunger, like a stealthy beast, still lurked everywhere and hid, ready to pounce.

Cornelius had heard of a bakery in Halbstadt that still sold the heavy, solid rye bread to those who could afford it. He became determined to be the one who would bring home the taste of something his family had almost forgotten. He could ride the mail wagon one way but would have to walk back. The bigger question was how to pay for it. After much soul searching, he decided to offer for trade a masterfully-crafted leather wallet given to him by his paternal grandfather when he was young. The family watched him leave with his treasured possession, with fear for his safety and doubt for his strength.

The day dragged on as they awaited his return.

Maria's words tumbled out after she had long held them inside for fear of causing more anxiety. "We should not have let him go. Someone could steal his wallet or the bread. It's not worth his life."

David tried his best to comfort and encourage her. "He will be fine, even if he doesn't get any bread, and he will have tried."

The sun's last rays were slanting onto the garden bench when they saw him. His sagging shoulders and defeated look told the story. Where was the loaf? Had he received nothing in trade for the valuable wallet?

The small paper wrapped package he pulled from his pocket could hardly be called a loaf. Through tears, Cornelius blurted out his story. "This is all that's left. I couldn't help it, I was so hungry. I just wanted a little bite. I wanted to bring the rest home. I'm so sorry!"

His empty hands told the story.

Disappointment overwhelmed Tina, anger and fury, but the sight of her brother in tears, the boy who would have died rather than show weakness, softened her heart. There was nothing to be said, but the rush of emotion left her feeling empty and defeated. How could her parents shrug their shoulders and just carry on as if nothing had happened?

David tried to put it into perspective. "Well, I guess we won't feel too bad about having eaten your share of the supper your mother put together. Come, what's done is done. At least you are safe home, and no one stole the loaf."

Tina suppressed her indignation with great difficulty. Didn't her parents feel anything? Weren't they furious he had left nothing for his family, his parents, his little sister? How could they be so calm?

Maria gave Neta a few extra roasted *zwieback* at bed time and sat with her on the oven bench, before they said an early goodnight.

Tina watched them go, then hurried off to tidy up the kitchen where, with choking sobs, the dam of disappointment burst. She had looked forward to seeing Neta enjoy her share of the loaf, something she had not had for so long. The sight of Neta's pale features and sunken eyes was her undoing. Her precious little sister was too young to suffer the ravages of hunger so silently. Fear for her sister's well-being blocked every other emotion.

In the days that followed, her parents smiled again but Tina's cup of sorrow was full to the brim and nothing helped to diminish it. Even waking on a sunny spring morning brought no relief. Sadness wrapped itself around her like a gray cloak; her time at the Kinderheim could no longer bring light to the darkness. She wanted nothing more than to turn her face to the wall and wish it all away. Only with sheer willpower could she put a foot on the floor and start her day.

Ivan was waiting for her when she arrived at the Kinderheim one early spring morning and grabbed her hand with all the strength in his slight body.

"Come Tina, I heard something. You have to come and listen. Come outside in the yard." The leafless trees held swelling buds and the tinge of green that promised growth. "Shhh, can you hear it? There it is again!"

And then she heard it, from a distance came the trilling, rippling sound of a bird, its song caroling on and on. "Ivan, it's a nightingale! It's my favorite bird! It has the most beautiful song of any bird in the world. It sings all year round, even at night."

Hand in hand they stood, letting the sound wash over them, Ivan's face beaming with happiness at the musical interlude, and with the knowledge that he had brought a moment of joy to one of his favorite people.

Like the first glimmering of light at dawn, the sorrow began to retreat, but it was not until Neta's sunken cheeks showed a glimpse of colour that, for Tina, the pall began to lift.

The last of the hoarded wheat was planted by hand as every plough horse had been taken, except one too old and weak to be of use in the fields. David's shoulders lifted, and his back straightened when the last kernel was in the ground. The burden eased even more when the field showed a whiskery carpet of green in the afternoon sunshine after a spring shower.

Days lengthened, breezes were warmer, and a tiny flicker of early leaves coloured the orchards. Evenings on the garden bench returned. Tina felt a whisper of joy when Franz Lentz, back from another deployment with the Red Cross, stepped through the lilac bushes. She could see famine had taken its toll; he was slighter, thinner, and more finely chiseled, but he still conveyed the same air of steadfastness and security. The kind blue eyes still held their measure of sadness, and their smiles for each other were tentative when they met across the distance.

In the villages, despite signs of recovery, all was not well. The autonomy of the village councils was slowly being stripped away. Hardly a day went by when the Soviet authorities didn't bring down a new rule or regulation. Religious services at the church were curtailed to one service a week, on Sunday mornings. Elders and preachers were questioned relentlessly and lost their right to serve as *Dorfschule* teachers.

Hilda was beginning to feel the heavy hand of bureaucracy as new rules affected farms, businesses, hospitals, and orphanages. Weekly inspections by the local Soviet caused fear and uncertainty. What were they looking for? No one seemed to know.

179

Workers shrank from their presence as the loud, unannounced visits upset children and staff as well.

A sense of invasion filled the orphanage as people who said they were family came looking for a particular child. They were looking for Nicholas or Alexey or Vera. Hilda was determined to ensure no child was given into the hand of someone with nefarious purpose. Proving a child's relationship to total strangers was almost impossible, and so far, only two children had been reunited with someone they knew. Two more night-watchmen were hired, but Dimitri was still on the job.

Around kitchen tables and on garden benches, pale, sunken-cheeked individuals, men on the verge of tears, women tight-lipped with fear, expressed their anger, despair, and hunger.

"They are trying to kill us all. Our grain goes to other countries while we starve. Ships arriving at our ports carrying a few packages of relief food are meeting shiploads of grain on their way to feed someone else."

"This is no longer the home we know and love. The time is coming when we will need to find a new home."

Still the grain requisitions did not end. The ones in power were blind or did not want to see.

CHAPTER TWENTY

A MYSTERY AND A PURPLE VIOLET

April 1922

HOW DID IT HAPPEN THAT NEITHER SARA NOR TINA WERE AT the Kinderheim that night? Over the years it was a question that haunted them both. Would they have been victims if they had been there? Would they have affected the outcome in any way? They would never know. They only knew that when they arrived that morning the orphanage was in chaos.

They heard the children shouting and crying as they neared the building. Where was Hilda, where was Dimitri, or Peter, the young night-watchman?

Tina shivered. When she walked in the door, a coldness seemed to surround her. Was it the chilly spring air or the atmosphere of calamity? The children clung together, some wailing with fear, others huddling on their platform beds, the only port in a storm.

They found Hilda in her office, slumped behind her makeshift desk, her nightclothes soaked with blood. Fear had become a familiar emotion to both Tina and Sara, but the terror they felt when they saw the state of their friend was beyond chilling. A gash on the back of her head had caused the heavy bleeding, but she was alive! The night-watchman, Peter Enns, had not fared well, either. Neighbours who arrived to lend a hand found him in the backyard, unconscious and bleeding. This was more than a break-in, this was attempted murder.

Later, Tina tried to remember the sequence of the events of the morning. David and Maria, the neighbours, two village workers, and many others arrived to help. When Tina heard Franz's solid footsteps approaching, she felt the load slip from her shoulders. His medical experience on the war train with the Red Cross meant he could tend to Hilda's injuries. Young Peter was taken to rest at the nearest home until his parents came for him.

Though Hilda was confused and unsure of what had happened, the memories began to surface. "I heard something in the night, I thought one of the children was up, but the sounds came from my office. I'm not sure what happened then, I went into my office and that's all I remember."

The questions flew thick and fast. "Should we take you to a doctor? Did you see anyone? Did you hear anything? Is anything missing? How are you feeling?"

So many questions, so few answers. "Are the children alright? I don't need a doctor; just let me rest for a while. Can you tell Dimitri I need to see him?"

The group exchanged glances and decided to let her rest before telling her Dimitri was nowhere to be found.

The children were silent now and clung to their nearest workers. They asked no questions.

Later Tina remembered Symon had been in the orphanage that night and, as an older child, might have heard or seen something the others hadn't. Tina found him outside, sitting in his favorite spot, under the budding willow bush, his head propped in his hands.

"Symon, did you hear or see anything last night? You know Hilda was quite badly hurt. She'll be alright, but we are wondering where Dimitri is and what happened. Did you hear anything at all?"

Symon was never one for idle chatter, but his dark eyes flashed when Tina questioned him. "I didn't hear anything! I didn't do anything! I didn't take any money!"

Tina was totally taken aback, "Symon, what money? No one is saying you took anything! Why would you say that?"

"People who break in always take something. Money is what they want." Symon shot Tina an angry look and turned to head out into the greening apple orchard on the edge of the village. Tina was totally mystified by the conversation and called out to Symon to come back, but he ignored her.

Back at the Kinderheim the children had calmed down, but the adults couldn't shake the sense of catastrophe. Franz stayed to keep an eye on Hilda as she slept. For both Tina and Sara, it was a burden shared.

When Hilda woke, she demanded to be taken to her office and the desk with its over-stuffed drawers. Her goal was to find a small metal box hidden at the rear of a drawer. She scattered papers in all directions as she rummaged.

"It's gone! The money from the council for this month, it's all gone! Where is Dimitri, why isn't he here?"

Sara knew she had to be the one to break the news. "Hilda, Dimitri isn't here. We've looked all over for him. He wasn't here when we got here this morning. No one knew where he could have gone."

Franz continued, "There is worse news, young Peter was severely injured trying to protect this place."

Hilda's face blanched and took on the traumatized look of her early days at the Schroeder house. Then she shot Sara and Tina another one of her accusatory looks. "You think Dimitri did this, hurt me and took the money and fled, don't you? You never trusted him. He'll be back. Just wait and see. He would never have hurt me, or Peter."

Hilda sat still amid the destruction of her office, for once defenseless and overwhelmed and not knowing where to turn. After long moments of silence, she turned to Tina and Sara. "I have to go see how Peter is. Can you help me clean up and get dressed?"

Though they tried to dissuade her, there was no changing her mind. With Franz and Tina's help she made the trip to Peter's parents' home, but even the short trip in the *droschke* left her trembling and shaken. Hilda breathed a huge sigh of relief when his parents assured her, with time he would recover.

Tina and Sara gave Hilda their own words of comfort, assuring her they believed Dimitri would soon be back, but underneath there were guilty doubts. They assured her the children were being looked after with the help of several women from the village. Tina and Sara filled in as best they could. Hilda seemed interested only in finding Dmitri or the missing money, wandering aimlessly around the building, searching, searching.

Franz reported the theft to the village Soviet knowing nothing would be done, but still feeling they should be informed. He was told it would be investigated.

The days passed without any sign of Dimitri. Symon had only returned once after Tina questioned him about the break-in, and then left again. Ivan seemed a little lost without his brother, but without the panic that had filled him the last few times he had gone.

Tina questioned Ivan, "Do you know where Symon is? Did he tell you where he was going?"

Ivan seemed reluctant to talk about his brother's whereabouts, but finally admitted to Tina. "He said he was going to Vasily and Marya's house to see if our mother has come back. He said I shouldn't tell anyone."

Tina shuddered to think of Symon, a thirteen-year-old boy, trying to find his way in a world of risk and peril, without protection, without food or shelter, in search of the one person in his life who truly mattered.

That evening, she spoke to Franz about her concern for Symon's welfare and her worry for the Kinderheim. "He's too young to be wandering around the countryside with no one to take care of him. And I don't know what will happen if Hilda doesn't recover from this incident. The Kinderheim needs someone to make the decisions."

In the weeks that followed, Franz's strength held up the faltering fortifications of the Kinderheim. He often came to check on Hilda's wound and to see if anyone had heard anything of Dimitri's whereabouts. He intervened on Hilda's behalf to the Blumenau Council who promised to replace the missing money, so vital to the care and feeding of the children.

The spring sunshine warmed the family's garden bench refuge. More and more often, Tina and Franz found periods of time to be alone. Around them, spring flowers, yellow Stars of Bethlehem, blue cornflowers and purple periwinkle blossoms fluttered in the breeze. A rope swing put up for Neta swayed under the over-reaching branches of an oak tree. A choir of bird calls filled voiceless pauses.

They sat there one evening as the golden-hued darkness of evening was closing in, and floral fragrance filled the air. Franz picked a tiny purple violet from the mass at his feet and handed it to Tina. The moment lingered, and Tina felt something new, a smile, a jolt of joy at the touch of his warm hands. No words yet, just a gentle touch and a glance across the blossoms. She tucked the tiny flower into her roomy apron pocket and smiled her casual thanks. Best not to read too much into a friendly gesture.

She told Franz of her greatest concern. "Ivan told me Symon has gone home to find his mother."

"Do you know where his home is?"

"Ivan knows the name of the town. Symon taught him a little rhyme about the name of the village. Nolgowka, Nolgowka, Nolgowka, near Tokmak, Tokmak, like a clock. He must have wanted to make sure his little brother would not forget where he came from." Tina's voice quavered as she thought of Symon searching for a mother he would probably never find.

Franz was more familiar with the Russian villages. "I think I know where that is. It's quite a distance. Does Symon even know how to get there? Tina, you realize I can't go looking for him. My mother is alone with two of the grandchildren, I can't leave her now. It would mean a two- or three-day trip, even if I could find him."

Tina nodded, knowing he was right. Relief mixed with a sense of guilt as she admitted to herself, she didn't want him to leave.

At home, she lay the tiny violet between the fragile pages of the small, leather-bound *Gesangbuch* which, in better times, she had always carried to choir practice. Years later, if she had been alive to hear it, someone who would have addressed her as Great-grandmother would wonder aloud at its presence.

The Kinderheim situation stumbled along. Hilda recovered slowly, but with little energy or enthusiasm for anything or anyone.

Tina and Sara, along with other village workers, spent time keeping a semblance of order at the orphanage. No word was heard from Dimitri. Weeks passed, and Symon did not come back.

Strangely, Ivan rarely talked about his brother except to say he had gone to Nolgowka to find their mother.

CHAPTER TWENTY-ONE

WE CAN ONLY HOPE

Spring 1922

PLANTING SEASON WAS OVER. DAVID HAD MANAGED TO PLANT most of his thirty-two *dessiatine* of land using the grain he had stored for seed.

Now, some of the remaining wheat could be ground by hand into a rough flour to make pancakes, just a few at a time. Maria found a jar of watermelon syrup and though it was dusty with age, everyone was excited to garnish the solid pancakes with the unexpected sweetness. Neta's thin, china-doll cheeks began to lose some of their sculpted delicacy. Cornelius's gaunt thinness still caused Tina and her parents concern, but early spring vegetables were taking the edge off hunger.

Rain, though not plentiful, soaked the fields often enough to encourage the tiny dusty seeds to take hold and flourish.

David, Franz and Cornelius, in subdued voices, discussed the serious situation in their country. David's voice had lost its jovial, commanding tone; there was a quaver, a frailty in his voice and in his body. His always slender hands were wrinkled, every bone outlined. The weight of his beloved country seemed to rest on his shoulders.

"This famine is far from over. We are the fortunate ones; our gardens are growing, our fruit trees are blooming, our grain has come up. We may not have enough, but at least we have something."

Franz agreed. His memory of the horror of the cities still haunted him. "What about all those that have none of that? All I can see is more death. If prayers are needed, now is the time. How will our country survive one more winter?"

Cornelius saw despair on his stepfather's face as he pulled another notice from his jacket pocket.

"We need more than prayer. This is another requisition for grain . . . to be filled as soon as we have harvested! This government is killing its people—deliberately! Asking for requisition after requisition so they can sell the wheat that should be going to feed our hungry!" David's voice took on an almost panicked tone. "Selling it overseas and starving its own people! How can they do such things?"

No one had an answer. For long moments the three sat, hearing only the rhythmic ticking of the pendulum clock and David's sigh of resignation as he tore the requisition in half, leaving it ignored on the kitchen table.

Cornelius pieced the torn halves together, studied them for several moments as if affirming their contents, then crumpled the pieces and threw them into the kitchen stove.

Like his older brother had done, he was searching for solutions. "We need to plant as much as we can of whatever we have seed for, even if it's just beans or turnips. At least we can help the poor in our villages and provide soup kitchens with something. The orphanage never seems to have enough of anything."

David nodded his agreement, but Cornelius knew it was mainly acknowledgement of his statement. His words confirmed what they all felt.

"What we need is wheat. By requisitioning our wheat, they are taking the bread from our table. If only they would let us keep enough grain to feed our people."

What else was there to be said? The group sat silent, hopeless.

Franz finally broke the stillness with one more piece of news. "There is one other thing we have to deal with. The Blumenau Council has received notice that from now on the local Soviet will be overseeing all organizations, including hospitals, orphanages, schools and churches. Who knows what that means? Whether these institutions will be closed, moved or administered by other workers, this is bound to affect our Kinderheim."

"Well, we should not be surprised. We had many warning signs this was going to happen." David's words were an expression of everyone's thoughts.

Around kitchen tables everywhere in the village, the news brought anger, rage and helplessness.

Sara and the other workers expressed their anxiety at not knowing what to expect. They did not have to wait long to find out. The Kinderheim was one of the first to feel the effects: more inspections, warnings, visits from members of the Village Soviet, all pointing to some radical change. The summer sunlight pouring onto the walls of the orphanage failed to lighten the mood.

Tina, Sara, and the others worked tirelessly to bring some enjoyment into the children's lives. Tina taught them the Little Hedgehog song that Ivan knew so well. Days out in the warm sunshine gave tanned bodies a look of health and they were reenergized with more plentiful food.

Ivan asked a few questions about the return of Symon, but no one had answers for him, and he soon stopped asking.

The days of balmy breezes and large puffy clouds, sailing along the grain-yellow steppes, went by all too quickly. Blumenau had survived one season of hunger, but another threatened; although dark clouds filled the skies, none held rain. Every household was busy with laying up food for the coming season. The orphanage struggled along as best it could. Hilda was present in body, but far away in spirit, and hardly seemed concerned when the Blumenau Council warned of coming change.

The family were seated around the kitchen table one evening when Franz had information about the Kinderheim to share.

"Mr. Thiessen passed on a message from the Blumenau Council. The local Soviet is giving them thirty days to get the Kinderheim running properly, whatever properly means. After that they will be making some changes. Mr. Thiessen thinks they will be shutting it down or moving it to another community under Soviet control. More and more rules are being instituted. All new workers must be hired by the Soviet. He thinks Hilda will soon be replaced."

Tina expressed all their concerns. "What about the children?"

Her family knew her real concerns were, *what about Ivan? where will Ivan go? who will take care of Ivan?*

Franz couldn't answer that question. As usual, hopeless looks and silence ensued. The light-hearted, happy family discussions were becoming rarer.

Then Dimitri returned! Late one afternoon while the children were at their supper, without any warning or even a knock on the door, he was there—thinner, disheveled, and dirty. The children were the first to see him. Their excited shouts of "Dimitri! Dimitri!" brought everyone to their feet.

Tina and Sara froze at the sight of the ghostly figure and were shocked by the state he was in, but they were more shocked still by Hilda's reaction. Like the Hilda of old, she flew across the room and in an instant was wrapped in the arms of the emaciated figure. The children watched with fascination as the two rocked back and forth, locked in an endless embrace. Tina and Sara were not used to public displays of affection and looked away with embarrassment. But for the first time in weeks, the light was on in Hilda's eyes.

The children's questions were all for Dimitri. "Where have you been? How come you've been gone so long?"

The workers, including Tina and Sara were also full of questions, but reluctant to ask.

Hilda intervened on his behalf. "We'll have to save the questions for later. I think Dimitri needs time to clean up and have some food and rest." The two spent time in Hilda's room and Dmitri emerged refreshed, clean, and neatly dressed.

Over the next few days, David and Maria and members of the Blumenau Kinderheim Council came, also hoping to get answers to the many questions they had.

Dimitri, never talkative, gave them the barest of details. "I have been in prison. They held me for all this time, never charging me with anything, just asking questions, questions, questions about the break-in at the Kinderheim. One morning one of the guards told me I was being released and to get out of there fast. So here I am."

Dimitri and Hilda closed ranks. Dimitri was reluctant to answer any more questions about how and when he had been arrested. They spent long hours in Hilda's office. The work of running the Kinderheim was left to others.

Hilda's announcement several days after Dmitri's return came as no surprise to anyone. "We have decided to leave Blumenau. Dimitri feels it's very likely that he would be arrested again if he stayed. Any accusation, whether true or baseless, would probably mean a long prison term. We can't stay here any longer."

David expressed his resentment at the announcement. After all they had done for Hilda, this seemed like abandonment, leaving the Kinderheim ship without a rudder. "How can you just walk away from everyone, the children, all of us and your Penner relations? How do you know you will be any safer elsewhere?"

Hilda's dark-eyed look was focused on David. "We have waited years to be together. This is our last chance. Our relatives no longer have a say in our lives. It's better if you don't know where we are going."

"Will we ever see you again?" asked Maria.

Hilda's shrug was non-committal. "We can only hope."

CHAPTER TWENTY-TWO

LOVE AND A
BORROWED DRESS

Fall 1922 to June 1923

SUMMER DAYS SHORTENED AS FALL WAITED IN THE WINGS. Early one golden September morning, with fond hugs and handshakes, Hilda and Dimitri said good-bye to the children at the orphanage. Hilda clung for a long moment to Sara, who for the first time in their acquaintance, saw her friend's eyes brim with tears. With one last *Auf Wiedersehen*, and with no hint as to their destination, they were gone.

One departed, and another returned. Isaac came home on furlough. He didn't sit on the garden bench very often and when he did his family's efforts to draw him into conversation fell flat. Maria was just glad to have him always sitting near and included him in every discussion even though he barely responded.

With as little warning, Symon came back. Excited children greeted him with enthusiasm but stopped short of hugs and handshakes. There was something unfamiliar about him. His body had stretched, his face taken on a cruder, rougher look. Ivan looked him over carefully, almost suspicious of the person who claimed to be his brother. As with the others, there were no rapturous hugs or shouts of welcome.

Ivan just looked at Sara and Tina and announced, "Symons's back!"

Symon's dark eyes still held the brooding look inherited from his father, though he was friendly with the people who had saved his and Ivan's life.

Ivan asked the question everyone was waiting for. "Did your mother come back?"

"She's not just *my* mother. She's your mother, too. She didn't come back. Marya and Vasily don't live there anymore." It was clear Symon had no more to say on the subject.

Ivan seemed satisfied with the answer and asked no more questions. He also had little to say when Symon only stayed for a few days, saying his friends were waiting for him.

In the villages, not everything was ominous. The rules for church use were relaxed, allowing two more days a week of community activities. Evening choir practice every Tuesday was reinstated, as were Thursday evening prayer meetings. Such minor changes, yet they were ones that brought joy and hope for better times.

Choir practice was more than singing. It was the social event of the week, which brought the younger church members together in legitimate interactions. The mood was light-hearted as choir members made their way to the church. Tina blocked the worry about the orphanage and the fear of another season of famine from her mind for a fleeting time. A sense of serenity, long absent, crept back into her life. She was surrounded by her friends and for the moment, all was well. The choir had lost none of its musical ability, even after months of little practice. Smiles lit their faces, songs filled their hearts. Was it all a sign of better things to come? Was the heavy blanket of Soviet oppression lifting?

On the way home, darkness had fallen, and the glowing poppies and chrysanthemums beside the path were just a vague blur.

The touch of a hand on hers surprised her, but something familiar made her smile. Franz was walking beside her, and this was no accidental touch. It signaled silent questions: *Can I walk you home? Can I see you into your house? Can we let your parents know?* Her responding squeeze of his hand was the answer. *Yes.*

The garden bench waited; the fall days stretched warm before them. It was time to plan, time to become better acquainted, time to hope.

The summer reprieve from food shortage was all too brief. Soon, news of starving children and dying elderly became daily fare, as famine again rolled over the land. Lack of food weakened those left behind, and disease laid claim to anyone unfortunate enough to cross its path.

Oma Driedeger died, and along with her sorrow Maria felt relief that her mother would no longer suffer the pangs of hunger or pain. David's youngest grandson succumbed to whooping cough, the relentless paroxysms of coughing that left a child weak and gasping for breath. After a golden fall of hope, a grey winter shroud of sadness hung over the Schroeder home.

It was a rare day when someone they knew didn't have a sad story to relate. The neighbour's infant daughter lived only a few hours and silently passed away in the night. Isaac's friend, Wilhelm, contracted cholera and died after suffering horribly. Epidemics of typhus swept through villages and left behind grief and despair. Would it ever end?

In December, the Village Soviet gave notice that the Kinderheim would be closed on January 30th, 1923. The children would be moved to an orphanage in Tokmak.

The Kinderheim already seemed empty, even though most of the children still lived there. Tina and Sara came to work to find many of the village workers they knew had been let go, replaced with Russian workers unfamiliar to them.

Tina received permission to occasionally allow Ivan to come home with her to sleep. The little boy's eyes widened as he saw the palatial residence his friend lived in. Every day there was food on the table. What more could one ask?

Maria apportioned what little was left of the hoarded food supplies from the secret place and passed them on to the needy in the community. Packages containing rice, beans, dried fish and fruit, sugar and oatmeal continued to arrive from American and Canadian churches and synagogues and were passed on to the poorest and the hungriest. Slowly, the back of the famine was broken.

The date for the closing of the orphanage came and went, but Tina knew the time was coming, whether today or tomorrow, that Ivan would be moving on, away from her care.

On a warm day in late March the garden bench was occupied. David and Maria sat sedately in the middle with Franz and Tina at each end. From the front room window, Sara and Neta covered their secret smiles and peeked through the curtains.

Talkative Franz was unusually silent, and Tina wondered if he had changed his mind until, after several false starts, the words came out. "Tina and I have become good friends this last year and after praying about it we feel it's God's will for us to be engaged and married. I am asking for your blessing and her hand in marriage."

David and Maria as one assured them, "Well, it's about time! Yes, you have our blessing. We are so happy for you." Tina hugged her parents, while Franz, gleeful with relief, shook hands with both.

He and Tina sat together now, side by side at their own end of the bench. They were a couple. The banns would be read, and the world would know they belonged together.

The celebration continued indoors, with coffee made from roasted barley seeds and tiny *pfeffernuesse* cookies saved for special occasions. Sara and Neta, and even Isaac and Cornelius, wished them well as they teased Franz that his secret intentions were known by everyone except Tina.

That night Tina dreamed the dream that had haunted her nights for so long. Again, she stood at the top of the long hill with dark clouds swirling at the bottom. Again, she was compelled to step onto the hill to begin the long descent. Again, her steps lengthened as the grade grew steeper. Faster and faster she moved, down, down, and there was no stopping until finally, the motion carried her to a crashing halt on the rocky soil.

She woke with the racing of her heart and the gasping breaths that had become so familiar. Question after question dominated her thoughts, keeping sleep away. *What had she done? What would happen now? Where would they live? What would Tante Lentz say? Did she love this man enough to leave her family home?*

She forced herself to look alert and ready to face the day when she went into the kitchen the next morning to help with breakfast.

Her mother's appraising glance took it all in. "Didn't you sleep well last night? You still look tired." A lump formed in Tina's throat, as after a long silence her mother continued, "It's a lot to take in, isn't it?"

To Tina's horror her lip began to quiver uncontrollably. Since the famine, no matter how hard she fought to contain her emotions, they swept her away at a moment's notice.

Maria's question meant she understood her daughter's hesitation. "Do you love him?"

Not trusting her cracking voice, Tina nodded a wordless yes.

"Do you believe he loves you?"

A smile crept in past the threatened tears. "Yes, I believe he loves me."

A rare hug connected mother and daughter. "Then everything will be all right. He's a good man. He'll take the best care of you he can."

Tina was to remember the conversation later, when so much strife divided them.

Spring 1923

The banns were read in church three Sundays in a row, announcing the pair as engaged, off-limits to everyone else. With the enthusiastic participation of her sisters, Tina and her mother began planning for the wedding. It would be a June wedding, with closest relatives only, a simple meal and none of the fanfare of most first marriages.

Meanwhile the Kinderheim was closing. The children were sent to other orphanages, but the question of where Ivan should go was still unresolved. Symon had been gone for weeks and no one wanted to send Ivan somewhere his brother might not find him. Tina was allowed to bring him home with her and when the last child left the orphanage, that is where he was. No one questioned his continuing to stay, and when the door on the building finally closed, Ivan had decided that he was very at home with Tina and Sara.

Tina and Franz were dealing with their own living arrangements. They would be living in Tante Lentz's large house, with a room to themselves, private in that it was at the far end of a corridor, away from the other bedrooms.

Tina occasionally felt Tante Lentz was less than enthusiastic about their coming marriage. "I don't think your mother likes me very much," she confided to Franz.

"She doesn't always like me very much either, but it will be two against one, so we'll be fine." Trust Franz to find humour in the situation, even if it was far from humorous to Tina.

"It's not that she doesn't like you, she thinks you are not big and strong enough to be able to run the household. I guess she would have been happier if you were the size of Hildebrand's Justina. She's as tall as me, and probably as heavy."

Tina playfully slapped her groom-to-be on the arm. Teasing was not common in the Schroeder family and she realized she had better get used to it. "Well, I won't get any taller, but I might be able to do something about getting heavier."

Franz said the right thing, "I love you just the way you are," and hugged his future wife.

Reassured, Tina put the niggling worry out of her mind and concentrated on preparing for their special day.

The day of the wedding dawned clear and bright, a June day in southern Ukraine. Tina, with the help of Sara and Neta, donned her wedding attire, a simple white dress borrowed from a friend, and a small lace veil held in place with a wreath of spring flowers. Franz had no ring for her finger, nor did she have any jewelry other than a small silver pin in the shape of a bird that her mother had managed to keep hidden.

She and Franz walked together down the flower-strewn aisle in the church, side by side but barely touching. Tina's bouquet shook slightly, but the nearness of Franz's body was warm through his loose Sunday suit.

The guests were few, many still wearing the gaunt and hungry look of the famine. The wedding *fesper* was far from what they were used to. The everlasting *zwieback*, cold, thinly-sliced ham, and *pluma moos*. No wedding cake, just a few less-than-flakey *schnetki* and *pfeffernuesse*, bland with less sugar and spice; limited fare but something for everyone.

The wedding gifts included a crocheted table cloth from Tante Lentz, a large, traditional, cloth-bound family Bible from Maria and David, and a teapot and two cups and saucers from the siblings.

It was hardly the wedding of her dreams, but as Tina clung to the warmth and security of Franz's arm when they left the church, she knew that together they could face whatever was to come. Though forever changed by what they had endured, the effects of losses and injuries hard to dispel, they were young, they were strong. . . .

CHAPTER TWENTY-THREE

THE DISTANT STORM

TINA REMEMBERED HER SIBLINGS' DISCUSSIONS AS TO WHAT their stepfather was to be called. Tina could hardly keep calling Franz's mother, Tante Lentz. Behind her back, Franz called his mother "boss", but that would certainly not do for Tina. Ivan followed Tina to her new home to visit whenever he could and referred to the old lady as Tante Oma. Tina called her nothing at all, but to others referred to her as Mama Lentz which would have to do until children were added to the mix, then Oma would be the natural next step.

Ivan spent more and more time with Franz and Tina. His future had to be dealt with.

"We have to decide what will happen with Ivan." Surprisingly, it was Tante Lentz who brought up the subject. "He's here most of the time. He may as well be living here."

Tina was shy about expressing her opinion but knew what she hoped would happen.

Franz just wanted some kind of amicable arrangement reached. "Well, what do you suggest? He's a good boy and old enough to help a bit around here. I think we should let him stay. He has no other family. Symon may never come back. I can't think of sending him off to some other orphanage where he knows no one and might not be treated very well."

Tante Lentz was silent and obviously considering his advice. "Do you both want this?"

Franz looked at Tina, knowing what her reply would be. "Is that what you want, Tina?"

Tina felt the wave of emotion that still overwhelmed her at the most inopportune moments. She managed to gain control and smiled her relief. "Yes, for Ivan's sake I believe we should let him stay."

Breaking the news to the boy fell to Franz. He was, after all, the one who made the decisions about the operation of the small piece of farmland still owned by the Lentz family. Ivan received the news with quiet disbelief until its implications sunk in.

His perpetual smile, like a beam of light fell on all his people. "I'm going to live here? Forever? I won't have to go to the orphanage ever again?"

After hearing the affirmative answer, he exploded into an eruption of joy, running from one to the other, throwing his arms around each of them. Even Tante Lentz received an unexpected embrace, startling her into a self-conscious smile and awkward return hug.

Asked which room he would like to sleep in, he chose Tina's, which caused an embarrassed silence and a quick explanation of how that room belonged to Franz and Tina and was too small for three people.

Thankfully, his second choice was the *kleinestubbe*, the little room close to the kitchen, just the right size for an almost-ten-year-old boy.

Tante Lentz carried on much as before, deciding the agenda of work and leaving Tina at times feeling like the hired help. Franz was oblivious to any difficulty, happy he had his new wife with him, and satisfied that the worst of life under the Soviet regime was behind them. For Tina herself, the adjustment to being married and the question of her place within the household, often left her feeling unsure and isolated.

The Kinderheim closed. The Schroeder household endured a double loss, the satisfaction of looking after the children and the loss of Tina, although it was only to the house next door. Sara missed being with the children but more than that, she missed her friendship with Hilda. She and Neta concentrated on the work of the household. In the summer it meant gardening, drying and canning fruits, cooking with the still-rationed food, and trying to replenish the goods stolen over the last few years.

Memories of almost three years of famine had taken its toll on the whole family. Isaac's absence only made things worse, worry for his well-being was part of every gathering and every mealtime grace included a plea for his safety. Cornelius felt his absence most keenly but sharing feelings was not a Mennonite trait, and he soldiered on in silence.

By Christmas, Tina's secret, known only to her close family, could no longer be kept. In late April or early May of 1924, Franz and Tina were expecting an addition to the family. Maria was the only one of the family who had known, although she did tell David, and soon the whole family was let in on the happy news.

Pregnancy was only discussed in the most general of terms, yet the thought of a grandchild, niece, or nephew brought joy to the household. For the first time in many months, genuine laughter filled the house. Neta and Sara discussed the fact they were going to be aunts. Maria and Tante Lentz put their heads together and searched the almost-empty bedroom closets for material to use for garments, bedding and other necessities of baby wear.

Tina wasn't quite sure how to feel. Sometimes, even in the bright light of day, the nightmare feeling of her recurrent dream brought tightness to her chest.

Menfolk were just glad that childbirth was strictly the women's concern. Worry for the future demanded far too much of their time. Every conversation focused on reports and often disturbing information, from various parts of the Mennonite Colonies, about the Bolshevik government.

David's worry lines seemed engraved on his aging face. "I haven't received a grain requisition in a while. Maybe we will be allowed to keep more of what we grow. What worries me now is the cost of everything at the Kolkhoz store."

Franz agreed. "What the government buys from us is cheap, what we buy from them costs us our right arm. What worries me even more are the rumours that this government is planning on collectivizing all our properties into one large state-run farm."

David was reluctant to discuss possibilities. "Well, for now the land is still ours and we have to manage it the best we can. There is no point in borrowing trouble. I believe the worst is over. We have to thank God for delivering us through this peril and go on from here."

Franz took comfort in his father-in-law's optimism, but like a distant storm cloud hanging on the horizon, was the worry that a government which had once caused the death of thousands of innocent citizens, would not hesitate to do so again.

January brought cold and wind and the despondency of a winter stretching on forever. In the Lentz house passage-doorway, one stormy morning, stood a ragged individual in a military jacket several sizes too large, his face covered, only his dark brooding eyes showing.

Tina immediately realized it was Symon, still thin and unkempt, the glowering look of his childhood more menacing. "Symon, what a surprise. Come in, come in. It's so good to see you."

Symon removed the tattered scarf and wordlessly reached out for an awkward hand-shake. He nodded a silent greeting to Franz and threw a quick glance at his brother.

Ivan took one look, then stepped back, drawing nearer to Franz and Tina. Symon hardly acknowledged his brother, just turned his unsmiling face toward Tina, reminding her of his early days at the Kinderheim.

Franz invited Symon into the kitchen and the warmth of the brick stove. He refused to remove the military coat but accepted several bowls of warmed chicken soup. Ivan watched him from across the room, from behind the safety of Franz's chair. The brothers glanced at each other, but neither spoke a word of greeting.

Franz handed Symon a hot cup of coffee, which the boy held in both hands. "Symon, where are you going on such a wintry morning?"

Symons answer was curt and barely understandable. "I've come for Ivan."

Tina and Franz exchanged alarmed expressions, not sure what they had heard. "What do you mean, you've come for Ivan? Where are you going?"

Symon's scowling look was directed at both Tina and Franz. "I'm going home to find my mother and I'm taking Ivan with me. He's my brother. He belongs with me." He pushed the empty soup bowl away and for the first time addressed his brother. "Get your coat! We are going! Now!"

Ivan turned a horror-stricken look on his brother and hid his face in the sleeve of Franz's shirt. A protective arm encircled the skinny body.

"Symon, you can't take Ivan out on such a wintry morning! Do you have any idea where your mother is? How do you think you will survive without extra food or clothing? We won't let you do this."

"He's my brother! I can take him if I want!" Franz felt Ivan's body flinch as it was struck by the hammer blows of his brother's words.

Franz tried to bring some reason to the situation. "Symon, have you asked Ivan if he wants to go with you? You can't take him if he doesn't want to go. You know that."

Fists clenched and eyes flashing, Symon sat up rigidly straight in his chair. He set the coffee cup on the table with an angry thump sending trickles of the brown liquid trailing across the table. His words to Ivan were louder than they needed to be. "You heard me! Get your things, we're going now!"

Franz's protective arm was around the frightened boy as he asked him the question, "Ivan, do you want to go with Symon, or do you want to stay with Tina and me?"

There was no hesitation on Ivan's part. Through a deep-drawn breath his whispered answer was clear. "I want to stay with you and Tina."

Symon pushed a chair out of the way and took several steps toward his little brother. "You'll be sorry if you don't come with me. My friends have lots of money. I'll be rich, and you won't have anything!"

Tina and Franz watched in bewilderment as Symon turned to leave the room, stopping once to look back at his brother. "This is your last chance! Come with me now or you might not see me for a long time."

Ivan's eyes squeezed shut as if fending off the shocking words. He stood rooted to one spot, his hand gripping Franz's coat, just as he had once clung to his big brother's shirt in the nuns' orphanage in Tokmak. There was no doubt as to his wishes when he shook his head and uttered an emphatic, "No."

Franz tried to stop Symon from leaving. "You can't just leave. It's cold and you need some food and some warmer clothes."

There was no stopping him. Without another word he was gone, slamming the door on his way out.

Ivan's body was trembling. He let Tina wrap her wool shawl around him and lead him to the warm oven bench where he sat silently for many long minutes.

Finally, the trembling stopped and keeping the shawl wrapped tightly around himself, he asked a single question of Tina, "Is he coming back?"

"No, Ivan, I doubt very much that he'll be coming back."

The answer seemed to satisfy him, and his face lost the worried expression, but he kept either Tina or Franz in constant sight. Still secured within the shawl, he played with his tiny red truck.

At bedtime, a cup of Tante Lentz's hot cocoa and a few freshly toasted *zwieback* were called for before he was able to relax and drift off to sleep, giving the couple a chance to discuss the bewildering events of the day.

Tina was anxious to discuss something that had been on her mind since Symon left. "Franz, are we doing the right thing?"

Franz was startled by the unusual question. "What do you mean? You think we should have let Ivan go off to goodness-knows-where with that rascal of a brother?"

Tina paused. Hearing the question put so bluntly shocked her for a moment. "I don't want Ivan to go with Symon, but I can understand why Symon wants to take him. The boys have told me bits and pieces of their experiences before they came here. Symon's life has been just one loss after the other. First his father being drafted into the war, his mother disappearing, and then his sister dying so suddenly. He was left with decisions no child should have to make. It's no wonder he wants Ivan with him."

"What are you saying? We should find Symon and tell Ivan he has to go with his brother? Out in the cold, heading into unfamiliar terrain, hoping to locate his mother?"

"I just want us to be sure we're doing the right thing. I've always felt that Symon knew more about the break-in at the Kinderheim than he told us. I remember asking him if he had heard anything during the night of the robbery. He told me he didn't take the money and I was so surprised because that was before we even knew any money was missing. Today he said something about money again."

Franz arm encircled Tina's thickening waist. "You could be right about that. He could well be involved with some criminal types. I hate to say it, but I think Ivan's better off with us than with his own brother."

After a long pause as they watched Ivan settle into sleep, Franz added the words that convinced Tina they were making the right decision, "He would have been very upset if we had sent him off with his brother. I think we're doing what is best for him. He's safe, sleeping in his own bed."

Tina looked up into the gentle eyes of the man she married. "That makes me feel better. You're a good man, Franz Lentz. I'm a lucky girl."

Part Four

ANOTHER DOOR OPENS

Could I be cast where Thou are not,
That were indeed a dreadful lot:
But regions none remote I call,
Secure in finding God in all.
Jeanne Marie Bouvier de la Motte 1648-1717

CHAPTER TWENTY-FOUR

THE FIRST YEAR

1923-1924

"THE FIRST YEAR OF MARRIAGE IS THE BEST." THAT'S WHAT Tina's friends, Frieda, Martha and others who had been married before her, said.

"Everyone pays attention to you," they said. "Your friends, your parents, your husband." She believed them and didn't understand their private little giggles and exchanged glances.

Looking back Tina could see the first year of their marriage really was the best. She and Franz wore their love like Sunday best, reveling in its novelty and newness, relishing every moment they could nourish it and help it grow.

Tina joined the closed and private club of married women. She saw the envious glances of her single friends as she walked to choir practice on Thursday evenings holding the arm of the catch of the village. Franz would have laughed to hear himself described that way, never having been aware his tall, blond good-looks were anything but ordinary. Tina knew better.

"Do you think the second year is as good as the first?" Sitting in the *kleinestubbe* in the Lentz house with Frieda and Martha, Tina could ask the questions she wouldn't think of asking anyone else.

Frieda laughed as she cradled her three-month old baby in her arms and kept a close eye on a rambunctious two-year old.

Martha made a breathless dash for her year-old daughter, who was in the process of climbing onto a cabinet loaded with small potted plants. "It is, if you like having babies, nursing babies, running after babies and washing babies' diapers."

"And hoping there isn't another one on the way." Frieda shot a questioning look at Tina.

Tina grinned sheepishly and said, "I admit it; you'd soon know, anyway."

"Late April, right?"

Tina was mystified, "How did you know?"

Both girls laughed at Tina's naivete. "Almost every one of our cousins or friends was pregnant within three months of the wedding. Some even sooner. That's life."

Pregnancy had already added another dimension. Tante Lentz still worried over Tina's thinness, going to great lengths to provide healthy food. Tina was encouraged to eat for two, even though her pre-famine appetite had not returned. Franz treated her with cautious watchfulness, having no experience with pregnant ladies. She often worried about her ability to take care of a newborn baby. Her experience was limited to watching her cousins and friends. They seemed to know what they were doing, giving her confidence in a mother's instinct.

Eleven months after the day of their marriage, came the experience that not all the advice in the world could have prepared her for. The reality, the pain, the helplessness, the panic, possessed her. Like in her reoccurring dream, she was compelled to step onto a long, steep slope and hurtle onto the rocky soil of suffering. On and on it went. In her dream dark clouds milled around somewhere far away; in reality they surrounded her, bore her away on billows of pain. When it was over, she read the news on the faces of her mother and the midwives.

The doctor, who had finally been called, assured her, "We tried so hard to save him, but your little boy is with Jesus, safe in a better place."

She clung to Franz, who had kept watch for two days and a night while she struggled to give birth. They held the body of their stillborn child and Tina wept, knowing their son would never feel the gentleness of his father's hands. Maria came to prepare the tiny body for the bed no had dreamed he would have to occupy. Franz carried the miniscule casket to the graveside service at the village cemetery.

Tante Lentz insisted her daughter-in-law was far too weak to take her place at the graveside, and secretly Tina was thankful, doubting her body could have made the journey. There was one thing she could do. Though her writing was shaky and uneven, the first entry in the family Bible had to be made. Under a picture of an angel watching over a sleeping child, she wrote the words, "Son, Isaac Franz Lentz, born and died, April 21, 1924."

The days that followed were dark blots in her memory. Day followed day of weariness. The doctor explained how after months of famine, the strain of pregnancy had taken its toll on her body. He recommended healthy food, meat and vegetables, bread and cream. He recommended exercise and fresh air, while she felt no hunger, only sadness and exhaustion.

Her friends and family tried to comfort her. "You're young. You will have other babies. God took him into His keeping. He is safe in Jesus arms." They succeeded in comforting themselves while she felt only emptiness.

It was only later that Franz told her of the terror he felt as the midwife tried to help her deliver the child. In the machine shed, far away from Tina's cries of anguish, he did something he had never done before. "I got down on my knees and begged God to save your life. I never really thought of the life of our child. He answered my prayers, He saved your life. I should have asked for the life of our child as well."

In that moment Tina felt love rush back into her body. Her heart broke to think Franz would feel guilt over the loss of their child. She couldn't prevent his grief or his pain, but she would not allow guilt to come between them.

She brushed back the curl of hair that had tumbled on to his forehead and caressed the worry lines from his cheeks while she held back her own tears. "We have to accept what happened as

God's will. I believe our little boy is in a better place; knowing that, I can be at peace."

Franz covered her hands with both of his. "I want so much to believe that someday we will see him again."

It was not until summer spread its bounty on the land, that the family watched as sorrow retreated and hope took its place. David and Maria let themselves laugh again as they saw the colour come back to Tina's cheeks.

The garden in the Schroeder's yard was once again crowded with people. Ivan and Neta sat in the grass weaving daisy chains for the dog, giggling at his embarrassed expression. Sara and Cornelius stayed for a short time before heading off to choir practice. Maria and David and the young couple preferred the garden bench. Even Tante Lentz joined the group at times.

Invariably, the discussion turned to future possibilities. David was adamant in his belief that life in their village was returning to what it had been before, before the revolution, before the civil war, before the famine. Better times were coming. The heavy hand of the Bolshevik government was lifting. A letter from Isaac brought good news. He let them know he had been discharged from the army and would soon be home. The family had come through the tribulations intact.

Franz felt an allegiance to his father-in law and wanted to take his side, but he could see danger signs everywhere. Why were more and more people talking of emigrating to the United States, Canada, or even South America?

Though the grain requisitions had lessened, the tax burden had increased. The local Kolkhoz store bought from local farmers at low prices but charged exorbitant prices for seed and other planting needs. Rumours of collectivization were everywhere. An undercurrent of uneasiness ran through the villages and was whispered about behind closed doors.

CHAPTER TWENTY-FIVE

TO STAY OR TO GO

1924

A KNOCK ON THE DOOR ON A SUNDAY AFTERNOON WAS NOT
unusual. David was surprised when he opened the door to a
distressed-looking woman, clothing unkempt and less than clean.
Her grey hair hung in straggly wisps around her gaunt cheeks.
It was not until she spoke, that he recognized Truda Penner,
Hilda's sister. She had lost so much weight David could hardly
believe she was the same woman who had been the stately lady
of the house at the *Sommerfluss* estate.

David invited her in and called Maria to greet their visitor.
Maria could see that this was no ordinary Sunday afternoon visit.
This was a person close to despair. There was something familiar
in the hazel eyes and the pinched mouth, and when David called
her "cousin" she recognized the woman who had pleaded with
her to take Hilda into their home.

Truda wasted little time on small talk. "Have you heard anything from Hilda? She's been gone for over two years now, and we haven't heard from her for more than four months. I thought maybe she would get in touch with you."

"We've had two letters from her, Truda, both shortly after she left. Then, nothing."

Truda clutched a white handkerchief as if in anticipation of a flood of tears. "Her last letter told me where she was living, then last Monday the letter I had sent her came back unopened and marked 'deceased'. I'm so afraid for her. I don't know what to do. You probably know my husband died shortly after he was arrested, when our winter house was taken from us. I'm alone now. I feel so helpless."

David glanced at Maria, a silent appeal for help. "Truda, I'm so very sorry for what you've endured."

Maria had no comforting words and relied on the eloquence of a hug to say, "How can I help?"

Truda's words were for David. "Is there anyone you know who might know something of her whereabouts?"

David knew there was little help to be given. "Truda, the only one I can think of is someone from the local Soviet who comes to our Village Council meetings. I might be able to ask him for help, but I have no idea whether he knows anything. Don't get your hopes up too high. I can only try."

Truda poured her heart out to the couple. "You have done so much for Hilda, and now I'm asking for another favour. I am so indebted to you. She's my sister, and I haven't always understood her ways, but I love her dearly. I'm so afraid for her now."

"Truda, I'd be taking a risk even going to the local Soviet. Most of us don't want anything more to do with them than is necessary. I'll do my best, but that's all I can promise." David gave her a hug and patted her back. It was hard to find words of comfort that were more than empty expressions of sympathy.

One thing they could do was provide food—a bowl of soup, zwieback, a cookie or two. They listened, they prayed, they offered a tiny measure of hope.

Truda expressed her thanks over and over again. David and Maria watched as she walked away to her temporary home at the Wall cousins.

Maria turned away while she was still in sight. "David, I hope she isn't depending too much on your help. You know there is very little you can do."

A visit to the local Soviet had to be undertaken with the utmost of caution. "I know. I can't just burst in there, demanding to know the whereabouts of a woman who fled the area under suspicious circumstances."

"With an ex-convict . . . " agreed Maria.

"Drawing attention to yourself with the Soviet is never a smart thing to do. I'll have to think this over."

Maria felt a sense of resentment building. "Haven't we done enough? I miss Hilda and hope she's safe, but putting ourselves in danger won't help anyone."

David's lips tightened, and he nodded in agreement. "I'll have to wait for the right moment."

The right moment came more quickly than he could have imagined or was ready for. A uniformed officer stood at the door early the next morning, demanding David present himself at the local Soviet at 10 o'clock sharp.

Shock left David silent. Could Hilda's situation have already reached the Soviet's attention? What was the purpose of this meeting? How long would he be gone? The officer offered no other information and was gone before he could ask.

Commands to appear at the Soviet were well known in the villages. What followed could be one of many things, mostly just questioning about some small breach of policy and then release, sometimes arrest followed by long absences with no outside contact. Sometimes, the worst happened, exile to a larger centre, imprisonment or even death. Maria felt a choking sense of fear. Please God, not David.

David patted Maria's clenched hands and gave her a reassuring smile. "I think if they meant to arrest me, they would already have done so instead of asking me to come to them."

As he left the house to begin the walk down the golden-leafed tree-lined path to his destination, she couldn't help but wonder, "Is this the last time I'll see him?"

The hours dragged by. Neta had gone to school as usual, unaware anything was amiss. Knowing appointments with the Village Soviet could end badly, but for Maria's sake wanting to keep as positive as possible, Tina and Franz came to offer support.

Sara paced the floor from room to room, finding small chores to keep herself busy, trying to keep her fear from transmitting itself to the rest of the family. Tears threatened, but she told herself giving in to panic accomplished nothing.

Cornelius spent the morning in the barn, cleaning, organizing, doing anything to keep busy. He wished Isaac was home; his brother always had ways to make time pass more quickly, even if only by giving brotherly advice.

Time for the midday meal passed without anyone sitting down to eat. The clock had just struck two when they heard him at the door.

"I'm here!" he called.

A wave of relief swept over them all as he entered the room. "You're home! Thank God, you're home!"

Signs of strain showed on David's face as he collapsed onto the oven bench in the kitchen. "I'm fine, they aren't going to arrest me. The questions were all about Dimitri. They say he was an officer in the White Army and may be charged with treason. They wanted to know everything I could tell them of the time he was at the Kinderheim, and if we had heard from him since he left."

David sat with his head bowed, his face covered by shaking hands. "I had to tell them of the letters we got from Hilda after she and Dimitri left. We will have to turn them over to the man in charge of this inquiry."

The family were shocked when he turned a despairing face in their direction. "They wanted to know where Truda was living and if she had been in contact with her sister. I couldn't lie to them. I told them of the letters she received and the one that was returned. They'll be questioning her next."

Silence filled the room. Sara sat close to her father, holding his shaking hands. Even Maria seemed at a loss for words, trying to find words of consolation, knowing her husband felt he had betrayed his cousin by telling what he knew.

"I told Truda I would try to help, and now I've made it worse."

"Papa, you couldn't lie to them. If they had found out, both you and Truda would have been in serious trouble."

David nodded, but they all knew he felt he had been disloyal to a family member. There was so little to say.

It was a relief to have Neta home from school, forcing them to put on a brave front, keeping everything normal.

After a sleepless night, David took the path to the Village Soviet to turn over the letters from Hilda. He reread them and realized they were little more than brief assurances that she was well. Dimitri was not mentioned.

It wasn't until he stopped by the Blumenau Council a few days later that he discovered Truda was being held at the Soviet for further questioning. No one had been able to communicate with her. The news hit David like a shockwave. The Council members tried to reassure him that as Truda had had nothing to do with Dimitri, she would certainly be released soon.

The incident had its effect on the whole family. Every look, every glance, carried the unspoken question, where is Truda? David became quiet and withdrawn, sinking deeper into a quagmire of guilt, while Maria and Sara waited for good news.

After almost three weeks of waiting, David and Maria received reports of Truda's release into the custody of her daughter, Greta. Although Truda had been set free after her long interrogation, it was said she refused to speak a single word about her experience.

Hilda and Dmitri's whereabouts were still unknown.

Though David was relieved she was home, his guilt seemed not to lessen. Tina visited her parents often, trying to distract them, giving them good news for a change. She and Franz decided not to wait to share the happy tidings that Tina was, putting it politely, "in a delicate condition."

Among the good news lurked the bad. On the garden bench, Franz listened as David revealed the worries he kept hidden from the rest of the family. "I'm afraid for the future of my country. I thought the worst was over when the grain requisitions stopped, and we were allowed to attend church when we wanted to. But I admit what happened to Truda, and to me, has me very afraid. Truda knew nothing more than what she told them, and yet was held for almost three weeks without her family having any knowledge of her whereabouts! She will never be the same."

The two men sat silently as David tried to control his emotions. "I am beginning to believe that now Lenin is gone, someone much worse is waiting to take over."

Franz agreed. "I heard if Lenin was the fox, Stalin is the bear. He stalks and devours anything in his path. It is said no one dares say anything to challenge him."

"What does our future hold? What will life be like for your coming child?" David distractedly picked some fallen leaves from the bench, his brow furrowed with concentration.

Franz sighed, reluctant to burden his father-in-law with his concerns, but knowing he could not hide his own fears any longer. "People are talking about emigrating. What do they know that makes them willing to leave everything behind their families, friends, homes, everything-- and go to a country they know nothing of? They don't speak the language, have no idea of what awaits them, good or bad."

David had few answers. "Many think our religious freedoms will be taken from us. Communists are atheists; they believe religion is a lie. I thought the situation was getting better, but I'm beginning to think it's going to get worse, a lot worse. I hope I'm wrong."

The two were silent for long moments, joined in worried contemplation of the question no one wanted to ask. "Is it time to leave?"

Leaving had never crossed Tina's mind. Although she was aware that some of her friends and relatives were going, her family was not one of them. Emigration was for other people. Her worry was for the coming child, for its health and for her own strength to survive the delivery.

Franz agonized over how to broach the subject. More and more of his acquaintances talked of emigrating to Canada, their reasons whispered to trusted friends behind closed doors.

Tante Lentz noticed her son's quietness, but carried on with her daily chores, keeping her thoughts to herself. Life had a way of imposing its demands, ready or not. She had faced famine and loss; she would face this as well.

Ivan had no thought of the matter and found ways to keep busy, helping Franz with the farm chores even though his foster father often seemed worried and distracted .

Reports of arrests, interrogation, imprisonment and exile became more and more common. Ukraine was held in the clutches of a monster who didn't understand the meaning of compassion or mercy. Franz could not help but think of looming disaster if what so many feared was indeed true. His blood ran cold when he thought of the future. Was there any choice?

How could he tell Tina that she would have to leave her nearest and dearest behind, turn her back on the tiny oasis of Blumenau and travel across the stormy Atlantic to an unfamiliar, faraway land? How could he lay such a burden on someone who had a baby on the way, and who was still recovering from the sorrow of losing her first child?

Many of their acquaintances comforted themselves with the hope that the privileges recently restored to them were a sign of better things to come. Farmers could work the land still left to them. Although taxes had increased, surplus wheat could be sold for actual rubles, though their worth was much reduced.

Others asked the difficult questions. Would this government work for the good of the people? Would the congregations be allowed to practice their religion in their own language? Would families be allowed to keep what they had worked for? Would the fear of night visits by secret police rob them of their sleep and security?

Maria's constant prayers were answered when Isaac, after weeks of delay, finally came home, changed, hardened, silent, and still suffering from the night terrors so common with returned soldiers. His family welcomed him and rejoiced in his safety, while trying to forget that only one of his service brothers had returned home with him. Was this to be the lot of all Mennonite youth, or would the government restore the Mennonite non-combative privilege? No one knew.

For Cornelius, the tables had turned. Now it was the oldest who needed help from his younger brother. He would be the one to offer comfort and encouragement, just as Sara had done for Hilda, with the hope that in time his brother would rejoin the family circle.

For both the Schroeder and Lentz families, an abundance of rain and a luxuriant growth of crops meant harvesting had extended well into October. Families rejoiced in the plenty, not only of wheat and barley, but of the garden produce that ensured hunger would not have a seat at the table.

Ivan was determined to help, handling the heavy grain sheaves, filling grain sacks, helping to move them from field to storage or flour mill. He watched as Franz worked on repairing equipment that had been sitting idle for years, handing him tools and learning how to use them.

The talk Tina had had with him on the garden bench one day caused him some concern. "Ivan, you know Neta has been going to the *Dorfschule*. Going to school is something everyone needs to do. It's too late for this year, but when school opens up again in January, Franz and I have decided you should go."

Ivan looked worried and not very enthusiastic at the prospect. "Do I have to go? I'm not good at reading and numbers."

"That's why people go to school, so they will get better at doing those things. You will get better too. You weren't good at speaking the German language but look how good you are now. At school, you can speak Ukrainian and read Ukrainian or German, whatever is easiest for you."

"I could stay at home and help Franz with fixing the machinery and taking the wheat to the mill. Or helping Oma Lentz with cleaning the house and cooking."

"Yes, you could still do those things, but you are almost ten years old. You need to improve your reading. Do you see all the books Franz reads? He had to go to school to learn how to do that. I will help you, and we can read books together. That would make it easier." Tina thought vainly of ways to make the prospect of school a little more appealing.

Ivan nodded his head with something less than enthusiasm but agreed to give it a try when school started in January.

That evening he took the toy truck out of its place and listlessly played with it for a while. He studied the folded and creased picture Symon had left behind. The young couple in the picture were still visible. The lady wore a simple white dress and held a bouquet of flowers. The man's dark hair was neatly combed, and a ribbon was pinned to his jacket. She didn't look very happy, but the man was smiling broadly. Symon had told him many times these were their parents, and Ivan believed him, though he remembered almost nothing of their existence. He refolded the picture and put it back in its place.

Tina was unprepared for the question he asked her the next day. "Are you and Franz my mama and papa now?"

Bringing the boy into their home because he had no one else was one thing, being his parents was another. "Well, because your own mama and papa are not here anymore, I guess we are your mama and papa now."

Ivan absorbed the information, while Tina wondered what he would ask next. She and Franz referred to him as our adopted boy when speaking to friends, even if he had never been formally adopted.

Ivan's next statement left her speechless. "I don't want to be called Ivan anymore."

"But why not? Ivan's a nice name."

"It's not a nice name. It's a bad name. Petie and Abram say it's a stupid Russian name! I don't like Ivan. I want to be called Hans. That's what Petie calls me."

"I think those boys are just teasing you." Tina was mystified as how to continue. "Let's not worry about it for now. We'll talk to Franz and see what he thinks."

Ivan's face took on the thundercloud look of his brother for a while, but his sunny disposition came through and he nodded and ran off to find something else to do.

He left Tina perplexed and unsure of the next step. Of course, adopted children took on the name of their adoptive parents, but she and Franz had postponed any decisions that depended on the legalities of adoption.

She remembered again how Neta had solved the problem of what to call their stepfather. Now Ivan was dealing with a problem to which they had not given enough thought. Would he also want to be called Lentz, instead of Danilenko?

There was no question of what her baby would be called; a girl would be named after her grandmothers and a boy after his father and grandfather. Only another three months to go.

The question of a baby's name was pushed aside when news of Hilda reached the villages.

Truda arrived one morning in a three-passenger *droschke* driven by her son-in-law. Maria, David and Sara were the only ones home. Again, she stood at their doorway, less haggard and unkempt, but tight-lipped with emotions kept in control. Maria and David led the way into the *kleinestubbe*, sensing that whatever was to be discussed needed privacy.

Truda seated herself, pulling her baggy gray sweater closer as if fortifying herself for what was to come, "Sara needs to hear this too."

Sara took the closest seat to Truda, dreading what she was about to hear.

"I'm afraid I have brought bad news. I don't know where to begin." Sadness lingered in her eyes, but her voice was clear and steady as she continued, "In the last few months Greta and I have managed to search out some information about Hilda and Dmitri's whereabouts. Greta's neighbour, Helmut Dirks, spoke to a relative, a Peter Vogt, who said he saw a man and woman fitting Hilda and Dmitri's description when they were all being questioned in the Lubyanka prison about five months ago. We spoke to Helmut, who told us Vogt was very secretive about the matter, but he described the woman and thought her name was Helen or Heidi or something like that."

Truda took a deep breath and clasped Sara's hand with icy fingers. "We have gathered as much information as possible from Vogt and a few other people who were willing to speak to us. We have no choice but to accept that Hilda died of typhus while she was held in that prison. We think she and Dmitri were captured trying to escape the country via Latvia. We have no knowledge of Dmitri's whereabouts. Political prisoners are usually sent to labor camps, or even executed."

Shocked silence, expressions of dismay, clasped hands and words of consolation. Sara sat with tears running down her cheeks, while David's arm encircled his cousin's shoulders and Maria tried to express their sympathy.

"Truda, I am so very sorry to hear this. All I can say is she is free from suffering. You can commit her to God's safe keeping. You know we loved her. She had such an amazing spirit. Nothing could stop her. She accomplished so much in her life."

Truda still sat unmoving and silent, as if all feeling had been drained from her. Her next words were for Sara. "She certainly accomplished more than she could ever have thought. Thanks to you, Sara, she had the chance. You saved her life. If it hadn't been for your care, she would probably have died in some mental institution. How can I ever thank all of you for what you did? I only hope she and Dmitri had a little time together."

Sorrow shared became sorrow eased. Experiences were recalled, even smiled about. Truda finally rose to leave.

"I have to tell you one more thing. Greta and her husband and two little boys are emigrating to Canada, and I am going with them."

Maria was speechless for a moment.

David's voice held only a slight tremor, "Truda, this is a shock. Are you sure this is what you want? What do you know of Canada? It will not be easy learning to live in such a different country."

Maria could not hide her dismay. "How can you leave your home and your friends and other family?"

Truda sat silent for a while, searching for the right words. "We believe that our life here will never be the same. I have nothing to keep me here. My husband, my siblings, all are gone. Greta and her family are all I have left. If they go, I can't stay behind. There, we can start over. We're working on getting our passports and the medical papers we need."

There were no words left to say. Hugs and tears were exchanged and finally, some tremulous smiles and farewell wishes. They watched as Truda stepped up into the droschke and with one more *Auf Wiedersehen*, was on her way.

CHAPTER TWENTY-SIX

KATYA

1925

"IT'S A GIRL! THEY ARE BOTH WELL!"

Maria and David could not stop smiling, though Maria's face showed signs of tears and David looked haggard after a long night of waiting. Franz remembered his fervent prayer for the life of Tina over a year ago. Now his prayer was one of thanks that his wife and baby daughter were safe.

The pilgrimage of the relatives began as soon as the two were ready to receive visitors. Sara and Neta celebrated their aunthood by declaring their niece the perfect baby. Isaac and Cornelius, as male bystanders, made their excuses. "All babies look alike, and we'll wait a while before we visit. Give Tina and Franz our congratulations."

Oma Katherina Lentz displayed her namesake with a sense of ownership that made the others smile. Little Katya announced her arrival in no uncertain terms, and friends and family declared she had been well named.

Ivan wasn't sure what to think and was surprised that one tiny girl could cause such commotion. He took a turn at rocking the cradle, but his theory that the faster you rock, the quicker the baby falls asleep, didn't stand up. Oma Lentz tried to teach him the finer points of cradle rocking, but mostly he avoided the job in favour of more manly work. His one concession to baby worship was fascination with the tiny fingers which wrapped around his when he touched them.

Tina and Franz were happy it was over and were amazed at the perfection of the person they had created–the tiny, shell-like ears, the pink perfectly-bowed lips, and the bright blue eyes that already stared intently at the world around her. While the grandmas and aunties lingered in adoration around the cradle, the father and grandfather left the rocking and cuddling to the women.

David maintained, "She will be a lot more fun when she can run around and say papa and mama. Little babies always make me very nervous."

Franz silently agreed, and in any case the baby seemed much happier with her mother. His happiness at gazing at little Katya sleeping in her mother's arms was tempered, however, by a looming threat.

Franz carried a burden, the outcome of which would echo through the years, affecting the future of Katya and any other children he and Tina might have. Emigrate, the word sat like a weight on his chest, feeling at times like it would suffocate him. Leave or stay? A firm decision made one day melted into wavering uncertainty the next. He kept it to himself, never letting even a hint of it touch Tina's awareness. Her concern was for the tiny newborn girl who slept in safety on her mother's breast. It was enough for now.

Signposts of perilous times ahead marked every facet of life in the once serene villages. The latest came via a visit from Elder Willms who told Franz and Tina of his experience during preparations for the 1926 conference of Mennonite Churches to be held in Melitopal the following year.

"We had to get permission from the Soviet to hold the conference. Final approval for the itinerary must come from them. We are expecting hundreds of delegates from Mennonite churches from the Chortiza and Molotschna Colonies and other areas of Russia. We were not expecting the Soviet Council to have the last word in every decision we made, but they have to be consulted about everything, even the location and accommodation of the delegates. The more we learn, the more worrisome this is becoming. Now they want their own representatives at every session."

Franz wondered, as they all did, "What if you don't agree with something . . . or worse, what if they deny permission? They control so much now, what will be left for us to decide?"

The answer was all too obvious. It was one more peal of the bell tolling the death knell of freedom. Was it also a warning sign that this was the last conference of Mennonite Churches they would be allowed to hold?

CHAPTER TWENTY-SEVEN

A STEP INTO THE UNKNOWN

KATHERINA LENTZ LEANED OVER THE KITCHEN SIDE OF THE stove, stirring the soup which filled the room with a tantalizing aroma. The fragrance brought Franz in from working in the machine shed.

"You may as well have some soup, now that you're inside." But rather than fill the bowls, Katherina sat down at the cloth-covered table, her signal she had something important to discuss. "Did you know the Kornelsens and the Wiebes have applied for their passports? Suza Wiebe told me Abram thinks if they don't go now, it may soon be too late."

Franz put down the newspaper he had just picked up. "Do you think he's right?"

"I just know more and more people are planning on leaving. They wouldn't make such a drastic move if they didn't have good reasons." Katherina's normally stoic expression became worried and serious. "I think our Heinrich and Jacob are planning on making application to emigrate. Why else would they have made the trip to Moscow without telling us?"

"I didn't want to say anything, but I think you're right. How do you feel about that? To think two of your sons are planning on leaving the country."

Katherina smoothed the table-cloth, removing every tiny crumb while Franz waited in silence in dread of what he was about to hear. "Maybe we should all go. I may be old, but I'm healthy and strong. Together we could make a new life for ourselves."

"Do you really think we should leave our home and country? I've thought of nothing else these last few months. I decide one way then change my mind before the day is hardly over. I've prayed about it and thought about it and talked about it with David and plenty of other people. I can't get it out of my mind."

Mother and son sat silent, overwhelmed by the enormity of what they were facing. There would be so much to do before they could even think of going.

In a rare physical gesture of support, Katherina patted her son's clenched hands, "Would Tina accept this? She has a young child to think of. This wouldn't be easy for her."

Franz stood up from the table and walked aimlessly around the room, stopping to stare out the window but seeing nothing. "I know that. I would be asking too much of her. I don't even want to think about it. She would be leaving it all behind–her parents, her siblings, while I'd be taking most of my family with me. Why should she have to do that?"

"If what we hear is true, you would be doing it for her and little Katya's future. If we stay and this government takes away our freedom to live as we choose, there may be no future. The Bolsheviks stole what we worked so hard for. It could happen again. I can't imagine our little Katya having to survive a famine like we did."

"The thought of it haunts me. I'm going to speak with David again. I think he agrees with me, but Maria will fight this with all she has. He'll be caught in the middle. I feel like I'm to blame, bringing them nothing but heartache."

Katherina Lentz was not one for hugs and hand-holding, just for straight talk and honesty. "You're not to blame for living in a country governed by pure evil, or for wanting to get your family to safety."

Katherina filled her bowl and set it on the table, but after the grace had been said, and after a few tablespoons had been eaten, she had one more thing to add. "I shouldn't even think about this, but what if a time came when we would not be allowed to leave, even if we wanted?" The thought silenced them both; it was the fear that lurked in the minds of everyone considering such a drastic move.

Oma Lentz had said what she had to say and was ready to spend a few minutes with her only granddaughter. "It's quiet in the bedroom, so maybe Tina will be able to come for some soup. I'll rock the cradle if the little one wakes up."

Franz's unseeing gaze was focused on the red geraniums blooming in their pots on the windowsill. Sunshine flooded the room. Everything seemed so normal, peaceful, safe. Was this the time to bring up the dreaded subject with Tina, or should he continue to say nothing, pretending all was well?

He had learned the hard way how easy it was to awaken a sleeping baby. In slipper feet he entered the bedroom, and before even speaking to his sleep-deprived wife, stole a quick look at the sleeping infant. "She's looks so peaceful when she's asleep."

Tina smiled and nodded and put her finger to her lips, hoping for once to a have a quiet meal with her husband.

As they sat down to their soup, all Franz's carefully planned words for broaching the subject disappeared, and he blundered into the thick of it with no heed for time or place. "Have you heard Truda is emigrating to Canada with her daughter and her family?"

"Yes. Mother told me."

Tina felt something inside her close like the slamming of a door. Had she been waiting for Franz to say the words: emigrating, leaving? Had she been holding her breath, hoping for the topic to pass by, while the dark clouds from her dream billowed larger?

"After what happened to Hilda and to Truda, they feel there is no safety in this country anymore." Franz knew he would have to continue, despite the shock he saw on Tina's face. "What if they're right? What if there's no future for any of us here anymore?"

Tina's look was almost panicked. "What do you mean, no future? We have a future. We have Katya, she'll grow up here and live where we live. She'll go to school and church and get married and have children of her own. That's our future."

Franz reached for Tina's clenched fist. "And what if they take all that away from us? We're seeing it already. They're taking away our right to decide how we want to live. They're closing our churches, harassing and arresting our elders and preachers. They're telling us how to educate our children. We're walking on eggshells, careful of saying the wrong thing. We can't even decide how to make a living. That's our future now."

"What are you saying? That we can't stay here anymore? That we should leave our home? I should leave my parents, my siblings, my friends, and the home I grew up in? Go to a country we know nothing about. Just leave it all behind?"

"I'm saying we should try to find out everything we need to know about emigration and about Canada and make a decision. I know I'm asking too much of you, but this might be our only chance. We have to find out everything we need to know. Can we do that?"

For Tina, every fiber of her being was shouting, *"No, I won't! I can't!"* What she heard herself say was, "I don't know. I just don't know." Was she about to take the first step down the nightmare hill of her dream?

The question followed Franz as he returned to the machine shed to work on the mowing machine. It followed Tina as she heated water for dishes and cleaned up the kitchen. It waited for them every morning and kept them awake at night. It intruded itself into the peaceful times of rocking the baby and stole the joy from seeing her first smile. It sat between them at the kitchen table like an unwelcome visitor and occupied their bed at night. It inserted itself into every conversation.

Franz spoke to friends who were firming up their plans, learning more and more about that faraway country, Canada. Tina listened when others spoke about it but asked no questions. Asking questions made it feel like leaving was an option.

Franz's work outside seemed to continue far longer than it might. Mundane chores kept them apart as avoiding the topic was easier than confronting it.

After weeks of indecision, Tina knew the time had come. She stepped into the darkened bedroom, watching as her awakening daughter stretched and yawned, the little face wrinkling in preparation for the new-born wail.

"Come, my little one. We're going on a journey; don't worry, it's just to the machine shed to visit your father." The baby let out one protesting cry then relaxed into the comfort of her mother's arms.

In the machine shed, Tina found Franz seated on an up-ended nail keg, staring at another piece of machinery that demanded his attention. His smile of welcome included the tiny girl she placed in his arms. She crouched down beside him ready to take the baby if he felt uneasy holding the squirming little body.

Neither of them spoke until finally, Tina said the words. "If this is God's plan for our lives, then I can't say no. We have to find out more and make a decision."

For the present, nothing more was needed. A strong man's face crumpled with emotion as he included his wife and baby in the circle of his arms. Their blended tears fell on the baby's downy head as, with that puzzled gaze, she watched her parents take a step into the unknown.

The days and weeks passed by with the subject never far from their minds, though Tina could not bring herself to speak to her parents and siblings about it. Little Katya learned to roll over and to squirm her way across a blanketed surface, already curious about what lay on the other side, and still the matter remained unresolved.

Not a day passed without some friend or church member talking about their plans for emigrating.

Tante Lentz's friends, the Wiebes and the Kornelsens, held an auction sale of furniture and equipment, the few animals they still had, and goods they couldn't take with them. Suza Wiebe was often seen in the Lentz kitchen, sitting at the table with a cup of coffee, tears flowing.

Tanta Lentz tried to comfort her when she received letters from her relatives in a place called Manitoba, where the winter had been spent in a tiny two-room house. The wind whistled through the cracks and the snow piled up to the top of the windows. The nearest neighbours were two miles away and loneliness was a constant guest. Tina overheard the conversation and shuddered. Why would anyone want to go there?

More letters were received. "Here we can say what we think. We hold church where and when we want. We can decide how to make a living. We can own our land without worrying someone will steal it or collectivize it. No one comes to our door in the middle of the night to take our father away. The police don't arrest a person for not agreeing with the government. Here, we are free."

Tante Lentz borrowed the letters, and read them over and over, one after the other, the negative alarming ones first, then the reassuring, comforting ones. Daunting or encouraging? Ominous or promising? Stay or go? Yes or no? Resting in her hands were the futures of children yet to be born.

While Tante Lentz struggled to reach a decision, Tina and Franz learned more of the country that could become their next home. Franz made careful lists of advantages of various destinations while Tina searched for answers to the endless questions which kept her awake at night. How could she tear herself away from everything that was near and dear to her? How could she face saying goodbye to her parents, to Isaac and Cornelius, to sweet Neta, who was just taking her first tentative steps into adulthood, and to Sara, the stepsister she had grown up with and loved as both a sister and a friend?

The walk through the lilac bushes the day Tina and Franz broke the news to Maria and David was the longest they had ever taken. Franz covered the coldness of Tina's hands with his own warmth. Her mouth was dry with fear over what she had come to say. She felt they must already know, or why were their faces so stony?

Franz's voice was strong and clear, but heavy with sadness. "We have made a decision. We are planning on emigrating to Canada."

Like daggers, the words no one wanted to hear struck home. Seeing her mother's flood of tears, listening to the recriminations, the pleading, came as close to breaking Tina's heart as anything since the loss of baby Isaac.

It was not until David, his arms reaching to pull his loved ones close spoke the words of comfort that reached even Maria's aching heart.

"We have to accept this as God's plan for your lives. Our love and His protection will follow you wherever you go."

CHAPTER TWENTY-EIGHT

TILL WE MEET AGAIN

A FUNERIAL SADNESS FILLED THE SCHROEDER HOUSE. DAY AFTER day Maria sat on the oven bench, rocking back and forth, tears flowing unchecked. Neta and Sara tried to comfort their mother, their faces blank with sadness, using words they themselves found hard to believe. What was there to say to a mother and grandmother who had learned her daughter and granddaughter were leaving, traveling halfway around the world to a foreign country, never to return?

The news spread through the village. All the explanations, the rationalizations, the excuses, the reasons, were given. All that was left was the fact they would never see each other again.

Katya's first birthday was celebrated. Through tear-filled eyes they observed the antics of a beautiful, intelligent little girl, who often looked quizzically at her grandparents as they vacillated between tears and smiles, knowing it would be the one and only birthday celebration they would share.

As a departure date was set, David tried to reconcile his sympathy for Maria at losing her oldest daughter with his understanding for Franz and Tina's concern for the security of theirs.

The Lentz family made the trip through the lilac bushes less and less often. The ties that bound them were loosening, Franz and Tina feeling the burden of guilt for the sadness they were causing, Maria and the girls feeling anger and resentment towards Franz for taking their loved ones so far away. Cornelius and Isaac felt part envy for the adventure their sister would be experiencing, and part anger for the grief she was causing their mother.

Ivan stood on the outside looking in. Where did he fit in this order of things? Franz and Tina and Oma Lentz would be going to Canada, Katya would be going with them. Tina had told him he would be coming as well, if that was what he wanted, but it was too hard to imagine that could really happen. His question was answered when a visitor arrived at the Lentz house.

An auction sale had been planned; the sale of furniture, household supplies, machinery, and odds and ends. The house was in disarray. People came and went looking for sale items.

The young man who knocked on the door and asked for Franz looked vaguely familiar to Ivan. He wore an odd mixture of ill-fitting clothing which hung on his gaunt figure. Franz felt the prickle of goose-flesh on his arm when he saw who waited on the doorstep.

Then Ivan recognized him, his brother Symon, almost three years older, less angry, less aggressive, humbler and more contrite. The two brothers stood staring at each other as if processing the changes time had caused, until Symon enveloped his brother in the first hug they had shared in years.

Ivan announced his news. "Tina and Franz and Katya and Oma Lentz are going to live in Canada."

Symon had only one question, "Are you going too?"

Ivan hesitated for a moment and then nodded, glancing at Franz for reassurance.

"His name is Hans Lentz now. He is our boy and is coming to Canada with us unless he tells us otherwise. He is on my passport with me as my son."

The memory of their last meeting and Symon's fury at Ivan's choice of where to live still haunted Franz and Tina, but the outburst of rage they expected from Symon didn't happen. He stood, expressionless, watching Ivan, seeing happiness on his little brother's face. Tina stood by, holding little Katya who stared, transfixed, at the strange man in their house.

The group seemed frozen in time as they tried to read the expressions on each other's faces. Symon finally broke the ice. "Ivan, do you want to go to Canada with Tina and Franz?"

Ivan nodded, almost fearfully, not knowing how his brother would react.

Symon's lips tightened, he turned away, his hands clenched as he stood staring into space. Long moments passed until he turned to face his brother. His face showed no emotion, and Tina and Franz let out shaky breaths of relief when he finally spoke. "I'm glad. You'll be safer there than here. Maybe I'll come to Canada to see you some day."

For the first time, Ivan's smile for his brother showed joy and excitement. Symon's ramrod straight posture relaxed as if a load had been lifted. With just a hint of a smile he glanced at Tina and Franz. He shifted his weight from one foot to the other and uttered the words he had rarely used before. "Thank-you for looking after my brother."

He seemed anxious to leave until Tina, passing Katya to her father, reached out to draw him into the room. "Spend some time with your brother. This may be the last time you get the chance."

Left alone the brothers seemed ill at ease with each other and could find little to talk about. For a few minutes Symon sat on the oven bench, the restless tapping of his foot the only sound in the room. Katya's babbling chatter from the other room brought a smile and a question for his little brother.

"Do you still have the picture of our parents? I'd like to see it again."

Ivan ran to retrieve the picture from under his bed where it was stored in a small tin box, along with the tiny, red and black metal truck. Symon examined the picture for several minutes then handed it back to Ivan.

"You can have the picture," offered Ivan. "It was yours."

Symon took one last long look, before handing it back to Ivan. "It'll be safer with you."

Symon was not one for long goodbyes or tears, just a clasp of hands, a farewell hug and he was gone. Ivan sat at the table, listlessly entertaining little Katya with the tiny truck.

"Symon said he will come to Canada someday. Then I'll see him again."

CHAPTER TWENTY-NINE

THROUGH THE RED GATE

1926

SARA, NETA, AND THE BROTHERS HAD THEIR OWN GRIEF TO deal with, but it was Isaac who reminded Tina that not everything was being left behind.

"Franz and Katya are coming with you, young Hans and Oma Lentz, they are your dear ones now. You are taking them. The ones who are left behind will always be part of you. We'll write long letters and send pictures. Our love goes with you, don't ever forget that. Who knows, maybe one day, we'll come to Canada to see you."

Such heartfelt words were unusual coming from her taciturn brother. Was this the first and last time they would hug and shed tears together? How could the prospect of lifelong separation be bringing them closer together?

Tina suppressed whatever doubts and regrets crept in. She knew there was no turning back. A wife's place was beside her husband.

The last steps were taken. The passports purchased, the medical examinations arranged for, auction sale held, tickets purchased. They were emigrating to Canada.

Tina's nightmare often woke her from exhausted sleep. The long hill still dropped down and down before her. Her steps still gathered momentum on the rocky grade and her heart raced with fear, but when she reached the bottom of the careening slope, she was still standing.

Days moved with lightning speed. Details of the trip were endlessly discussed. Leaving from the train station at Lichtenau, traveling to Moscow, then by train under the Red Gate and over the border between Russia and Latvia—the line between oppression and freedom. They would board a ship at Riga, Latvia, sailing to Southampton, England, from there via S.S. Melita to Liverpool, to board the ship S.S. Montroyal, to sail across the Atlantic, arriving in St. John, New Brunswick, then by CPR train to their destination in a small community in Southern Alberta, Canada.

Whirlwind planning, what to take, what to leave. Essentials: the family Bible, food for the trip, toasted *zwieback*, dried fruit, dried meat, clothing for winter, photographs, bedding, kitchen utensils, and household things.

Maria and Sara, with Neta's help, spent days cooking, baking, and putting together baskets of food for the day of departure.

The last few days would be spent with both families together. The Lentz house was bare and deserted, their belongings packed and ready for departure.

Maria and David hid their grief and their dread. This was a time for saying goodbye with no recriminations, blame or guilt. It was a time for hopefulness and encouragement. It was a time for silent prayers, for faith and trust in a loving God who would guide and protect.

Maria kept busy preparing food, occasionally grabbing Katya up and hugging her to herself until the little girl's giggles turned to struggles to escape. Her grandma and aunties couldn't help but laugh at the little girl's delight when Uncle Cornelius pretended to be a cat and meowed pathetically. Uncle Isaac, not to be outdone, lifted her high onto his shoulders and galloped like a horse. Everyone had their moments of turning away from the precious sights, hiding trembling lips and the tears that threatened to spill. Tears mingled with smiles, memories were unearthed, love was expressed.

David spoke the words, no doubt echoed by everyone who was being left behind. "Heavenly Father, we pray You will be with our loved ones as they travel across the ocean to a foreign land. Shelter them, protect them, see them safely to their new home, and if it is Your will, grant us all a *Wiedersehen*, if not in this life, then in the next."

One last walk around the village, when like many others who were leaving, Tina and Franz gazed at the buildings that had marked so many milestones in their lives: the school, the store, the church, the orphanage now empty and forlorn, the brick-lined fences and gates of neighbour's homes, the tiny grave in the deserted cemetery.

The garden bench in the Schroeder's yard was dusty and leaf-strewn, the rope swing dangling by a single cord, the garden paths un-swept. One long look to store the images, like sepia portraits, forever in their minds.

The time had come for one last church service the morning before departure. The last handshakes, the last hugs, the last shared tears, the last song, *Gott mit euch bis wir uns wiederseh'n.* (God be With You 'till We Meet Again.) The choir sang out loud and strong, only to falter and fade as the sadness of the melody reduced everyone to tears. Even the strongest, the most stoic, gave up trying to hide the wetness on their cheeks. Everyone was saying good-by to someone.

Then, it was time to go.

CHAPTER THIRTY

ON MY WAY TO CANADA

1926

HANS LENTZ STOOD ON THE THIRD-CLASS PASSENGER DECK. NO comfortable deck chairs here, so he stood near the rail as the S.S. Montroyal steamed her way across the Atlantic towards St. John, New Brunswick, Canada.

Katya was with him. He held her securely and shielded her from the breeze. He was the official childminder as seasickness, which lay the adults low, never bothered him or Katya. Katya, secure in Hans' arms, seemed unfazed by the movement of the ship, now it had reached calmer waters. She clung to her big brother and buried her face in his jacket when the salty spray hit her face.

During her nap times, Hans was free to roam the ship's hidden galleys and gangways, even though they were forbidden to passengers. It was easy for one slight, harmless-looking boy to make himself scarce when the occasion demanded.

The best part was the second-class passenger's deck, where, from behind a stack of lounge chairs, he could watch the rich passengers on their afternoon walks. There seemed far fewer than when they had set sail. Did rich people get seasick too?

No one paid much attention to him when he became brave enough to stand at the second-class passenger deck-rail and watch the whitecaps being whipped up on the rolling acres of water. The ocean was endlessly fascinating, its colours, its smells, it sounds, the taste of the spray on one's lips, the odd bits of debris that occasionally sailed by.

Later, he could never remember how it happened. When he reached into his pocket to take out the precious red and black truck, the picture of his parents fell out, and as he reached for it, a gust of wind snatched it from his fingers. He made one panicked grab for it as the tiny flicker of white whirled above his head and was gone.

He was never sure if the ocean breeze had whipped it from his grasp, or if he had just let it go.

When a deckhand came to question him about his passenger status and identity, he answered without hesitation, "My name is Hans Lentz. My parents are Tina and Franz Lentz, my sister is Katya Lentz and my grandmother is Katherina Lentz. I come from Blumenau, Molotschna Colony in Southern Russia, and I am on my way to Canada."

AUTHOR

AGNES THIBERT WAS BORN IN Coaldale, Alberta, where her parents lived after immigrating from Ukraine. She spent most of her school years in Coaldale and graduated from the University of Lethbridge with a B.Ed. in 1982. After an extensive teaching career, she retired in 2000 and now lives in the rural Lundbreck area, near Pincher Creek, where she and her husband raised their family.

Mother of three, grandmother of six, great-grandmother of two, Agnes is an avid researcher into the lives of her family members who lived through the tumultuous years of Revolution and Civil War in Russia, before their emigration to Canada in 1926.

When her brother, Peter Langemann took on the task of translating the dozens of letters received by their parents from the relatives left behind in Ukraine to face the wrath of the Bolshevik government, the door to the past opened. The language barrier was overcome and the signatures on the letters, the names on the back of fragile, discoloured photos turned into real people. They were her aunts, her uncles, her grandparents. Their experiences became part of the lore of Agnes' childhood. Her parents kept in constant communication with the loved ones until 1934 when the last letter arrived, and all communication ceased.

It is her hope that the lives of the fictional families in the book reflect the faith, courage and sacrifice it took for so many to leave the past behind and face existence in a strange land.

Printed in Canada